THE DIAL
BENJAMIN REYNOLDS

Transcribed by Rosalie Esmond Blizard

HERITAGE BOOKS, INC.

Copyright 1993

by Rosalie Esmond Blizard

Published 1993 By

HERITAGE BOOKS, INC.
1540-E Pointer Ridge Place, Bowie, Maryland 20716
(301) 390-7709

ISBN 1-55613-796-6

A Complete Catalog Listing Hundreds of Titles on
Genealogy, History, and Americana
Available Free on Request

ACKNOWLEDGEMENTS

I would like to dedicate this book (for Benjamin Reynolds) to all of his friends – past – and relatives – past and present of which I am honored to be one.

I would like to thank Mrs. John S. Magill, my aunt Dorothy, for giving me the diary, for without it there would be no account of this very interesting sea voyage in the year, 1840.

I would like to extend my gratitude to Benjamin for writing this journal and allowing me, the reader and transcriber, the pleasure of joining him on his adventure to South America.

To my husband, Paul, I give my heartful thank you for all his patience and love during my work on this project.

CONTENTS

ACKNOWLEDGEMENTS
iii

AUTHOR'S NOTES
ix

BENJAMIN REYNOLDS
xi

PROLOGUE
xiii

CHAPTER ONE
Ship "Roanoke"
December 31, 1839
1

CHAPTER TWO
Ship Roanoke
At Sea
January 31, 1840
9

CHAPTER THREE
At Sea
March 1, 1840
15

CHAPTER FOUR
At Sea
March 25, 1840
19

CHAPTER FIVE
Valparaiso
April 1, 1840
23

DRAWINGS
26 – 31

CHAPTER SIX
Valparaiso
April, 1840
33

CHAPTER SEVEN
Valparaiso
May 1, 1840
43

CHAPTER EIGHT
At Sea
June 12, 1840
45

CHAPTER NINE
Rio de Janeiro
June, 1840
49

CHAPTER TEN
Rio
July, 1840
55

CHAPTER ELEVEN
At Sea
August, 1840
"Homeward Bound"
61

Page 66
Portrait of Benjamin Reynolds
1840

AUTHOR'S NOTES

My name is Rosalie Ann Esmond Blizard. My mother's maiden name is Magill. Her full name is Elizabeth Carter McKaraher Magill Esmond. Her father, Kirk Wells Magill (1857–1931), was the son of William Magill, born on June 9th, 1811 (June 9 happens to be the day I was married 30 years ago) who married Elizabeth, called "Eliza" McKaraher on September 25, 1845. Eliza's father, Charles McKaraher (1796–1849), wrote a personal diary from 1843 to 1845. He is my great-great grandfather. I am privileged to have been given this diary and I am in the process of transcribing this journal for future publication. It is from the interest that it has provoked in me that I have decided to write this book. My Aunt Dorothy Magill, gave me this Journal and a year later found another diary written by a man named Benjamin Reynolds. By reading through my great-great grandfather's diary I learned that Benj Reynolds was a good friend of John McKaraher and Helen Rosalie McKaraher – son and daughter of Charles, and that in 1845, Ben married Helen Rosalie, who was a sister to Eliza McKaraher Magill, my great grandmother. This makes Ben my great uncle by marriage. Also, my name, Rosalie, it seems originated from Ben's wife. It is his Sea Voyage from Philadelphia, all the way around Cape Horn to Chile, back around the Cape up to Rio de Janeiro, and back to Philadelphia from 1840–1841 that I have written down (verbatim) for you to read. I found his sea account absolutely fascinating, not only because he was a relative but because of (contrary to his thinking) the eloquent way in which it was presented.

BENJAMIN REYNOLDS

As far as I can tell from my research, Ben was a single man in his twenties, when he took this trip.

By reading my great-great grandfather's diary I learned a little bit about Ben. He was a friend of the family. Actually, John McKaraher, my great uncle, was his best friend. John had a younger sister by two years, Helen Rosalie ,who apparently fell in love with Ben and they married in 1845. This is taken directly from the pages of Charles McKaraher's Diary:

"25th Sept. – Thursday morning my daughter, Helen Rosalie McKaraher, was married to Mr. Benjamin Reynolds by the Rev. Thomas Barnard, Pastor of the 3rd Presbyterian Church, corner of 11th and Pine St. at 7 o'clock in the presence of her father, mother, brothers, John and Jackson, sisters, Eliza, Margaret, Charlotte, Mary and Catherine, Uncle John Gethen, Aunt Eliza, Mary Bradley, Margaret and Maria Gethen, and brother – law, Wm. H. Magill, Eliza's husband, Cousin Josephine Mayer and William Brooks, a young man in my store, his mother, Mrs. Reynolds, brothers, Thomas and Edward. After the ceremony was over the Bride and Groom left in a steamboat for N.Y., Boston, and Albany. Mr. Reynolds is in the wholesale business in N. Water St. No. 11, one of the Girard stores."(An interesting footnote to this is something else I noted in Charles McKaraher's diary). "Mr. Benj Reynolds moved his store from No. 4 South to No. 11 North Water st. in 1845. It had 3 stories and a good cellar. His rent at the time was $600 a year. From every appearance Mr. Reynolds is in a fair way of property. He is(?) years old (he didn't know, I think he was 27) and she is 25 years old. May every success and happiness attend them."

The Genealogical Society of Pennsylvania, 1300 Locust St. Phialdelphia, Pa. wrote to me with this information:

Charles McKaraher was born in Philadelphia on 31 January, 1796, son of Daniel McKaraher and Susannah Dunwoody Hamill. He married Eleanor Gethen February 22, 1815. (This came from a genealogical survey on the McKaraher family). Charles is listed as having a "fancy store" in 1846 at 27 N. 2nd St.

Benjamin Reynolds listed as being a grocer on Water Street in the City Directories of 1844 and 1846.

In tracing the McKaraher family it seems Ben and Helen Rosalie had two daughters, Kate and Anna, who never married. It was interesting to note that in the back of the Reynolds diary the daughters height and measurements were written down. January 22, 1860:

Kate Reynolds – 4ft. 6 1/2 inches, round breast 27 1/2 inches, round waist 20 1/2 inches. Height of Anna Reynolds – January 22, 1860 – 4 ft. 1 inch, breast 24 1/2 inches – waist 21 1/2 inches, round head 20 1/2 inches – length of arm 20 1/2 inches including hand. It also said: Ben Reynolds 5 ft. 6 1/2 inches in stockings. The daughters were probably ten and twelve years old at the time. This is only a guess on my part as I have no further information on the Reynolds family.

PROLOGUE

On Board – "Ship Roanoke"
December – 1839

As promises should always be fulfilled, whenever it is possible for the promiser to accomplish it; and having promised to several of my friends before leaving my native land, that, which absent from them I would keep a journal in memorandum of the most remarkable and interesting things or events, which I might see, or should occur during my exile from home. I now seat myself to commence said Journal in memorandum with the intention of making additions from time to time, until the happy hour arrives when I shall be once more surrounded by those friends who are now present only in memory; should I ever be permitted to reach my dearest home in safety. In hopes that from the want of something better, it may serve to wile away a leisure hour or so and prove that although I am absent, I am not forgetful – – of friends at home. Those however, who open this book for the purpose of perusing my Journal must not expect to find its pages filled with high flown words or startling narratives; as like "Othello" — the author is but " rude in speech and little versed in the set phrase of eloquence." Yet by your permission, he will a plain, unvarnished tale deliver, and if not successful in rendering it sufficiently interesting, to induce the reader to accompany him through the many ups and downs he is most likely to meet with before his reaching home; he will enjoy the satisfaction of knowing that he has done his best, and with that conviction keeping an ever watchful eye to truth, he hopes to interest those of his friends who may be pleased to favor him with a perusal of the following pages.

Since writing the following pages, I have had the patience to peruse them and correct the most flagrant errors; but not all, and am perfectly aware of the existence of many mistakes and bad expressions, but those who read them must bear in mind, that this book is merely a partially corrected blotter, and as I am not disposed to copy it they must take the will for the deed.

CHAPTER ONE

Ship Roanoke
December 31, 1839

Once more in the short space of ten months I find myself seated in the cabin of a ship, and riding o'er the briny and bottomless deep, every wave of which is driving our frail shell still farther from my childhood's home, and those dear friends the like of whom I may never be permtted again to look upon - - but "Hope", that ever faithful anchor of soul, now whispers in mine ear, and seems to say in words which do not sound - - despair not - - for the future has little many a happy hour in reserve for thee - - and "Time" is ever on the wing. It will soon bear thee to thy friends and home. How blessed is man, that he can hope, and how wise is our Almighty Father, to prevent frail mortals from an in sight to futurity thereby granting us many days of happiness and joy - - which otherwise would be, but misery and despair.

Little did I anticipate, when in February last I bid adieu to friends and home, that in the same year I should be again called upon to leave my dearest Mother's fine side, and bid farewell to the shores of my Native Land, to wander forth a stranger in a foreign land to meet the cold from the heartless and unfeeling world whose greatest feat is to censure and condemn. To him who loves his home, the thought of its sweet pleasures and past times, are as dear to him, as life itself and may well compel him to exclaim - - that all the wealth of Eastern Kings have not the power to part the "Thoughts of home and me". Most of my friends will have learned long before my return; that we are now bound on a voyage to the Pacific Ocean on the west coast of South America. Our destination port is Valpariso, situated in South Latitude 33 degrees 01' and Longitude 71 degrees 37' west in the principle sea port of the Republic of Chile.

Our most fervent and sincere prayer will be that Our Almighty Father will in his infinite mercy – – guard and protect our gallant vessel from the fury of the winds and waves; and grant us a safe and speedy passage to our destined port and a quick return to the water of our own dear land.

To give a description of parting from my home, is not within my power; and the imagination must describe those feelings to which words cannot give utterance yet, perchance this may reach the hands of those whomever yet have been called upon to say adieu to friends and home and wander forth alone, friendless and unknown; who would like to learn if it were possible; the actual state of a person's feelings when called upon to perform this unpleasant task. To such who would learn my feelings; I know of no better manner of expressing them, than for him to imagine himself sailing o'er the Sea, in a ship accompanied by a number of friends and companions. The gallant ship is tight and strong, all retire to rest assured of safety and confidently anticipate that ere the mornings glorious sun has disappeared from the Western Horizon – – their favored barque will be safely moored in her destined harbour; and all the crew safely landed, with their friends ashore. With such fond thought all are now wrapped in slumber deep. Naught is heard save the tread of the watch upon the deck, the creaking of the rudder obeying the movements of the helmsman, the gargling and hissing sound of the waves as they recede from the vessels side, and howling of the winds as if maddened by meeting with opposition in the sails and rigging. The bell strikes eight which tells of the hour of midnight. The wind, which at sundown was but a moderate breeze, has been gradually increasing until it now becomes a frightful gale. The sea, which a few hours before was comparatiely smooth, is now roused to anger and is lashing the vessel with awful fury and roaring with maddened rage. The watch is called and all hands ordered aloft to take in sails in hopes of rendering the Ship more easy as she is now laboring hard. The sea is making a complete breach over the doomed vessel, already the work of destruction has commenced. Bulwarks are stone, the longboat has long since been washed away and the last wave has swept the deck of every movable article. The sails are furled after an hours long hard labor but still the vessel labors heavily. As a last resource the Captain orders the masts to be cut away. In a few minutes the work is completed, and crash after crash is heard, as the tall tapering masts fall heavily over the vessels side and are soon bourne away from those they have served so long. The vessel has now become an unmanageable wreck, and all the efforts of those on board, seem only to enrage the tempestuous elements and call them down, with increased strength upon their unfortunate barque. All that mortal power can do has now been done; and wearied man resigns himself to fate, indulging in the fond delusive hope of yet reaching the shore in safety, or being rescued from their fast sinking wreck by some vessel that has with stood the fury of the gale. Soon their eyes behold a new and far more fearful danger, as the vessel is fast approaching a reef of rock over which the sea is breaking with awful and frightful fury; to escape them is impossible, and to strike them is certain destruction to all. A shock which prostrates all on board, convinces them that their vessel has struck, another and another sea strikes the ill-fated wreck, and piece by piece is torn from her hull. And to make the work of destruction complete, she breaks asunder, unable longer to resist the tempest's strength. With the last and most destructive wave, her crew are washed from her, and dashed upon the rocky shore. Soon the dark looking spot which was faintly visible from the shore, now disappears and naught is heard but the roaring of the boisterous sea, as it dashes with a herculanian strength upon the cragged rocks. The long wished for hour of day break, at last arrived, and with it discovers a solitary being seated upon the highest point of rocks. His eyes upon the sea washed shore, he drops his head in agony and despair for naught meets his eye, but the raging sea, and a few pieces of wood which speak volumes to his soul. They are the only remains of the unfortunate vessel which has bourne him to this place he at present occupies. He looks, but look in vain, in hopes of meeting the gaze of some one of his comrades of the previous night; but none meet his eye, and he finds himself the only soul who has been spared, of the crew of their once gallant ship. There he is placed upon a barren island in the midst of the broad, deep sea. Entirely alone, no help, no friends, no kind protecting hand is near to administer to his many wants, or to soothe his sorrows. He wanders forth an outcast from the world. Hope at last deserts him. Despair takes possession of his soul, and from the most inward man – – he exclaims – – "Oh, Death, where is thy sting ?" Let the reader imagine himself, the solitary being, who is here left to perish, who in a moment of fancied security and repose, is suddenly snatched from the fond embrace of friends, and the company of all he holds dear on earth. All; all, are gone, and he is left alone. Despair has claimed possession of his soul; and he counts reflection the embrace of death. I repeat; imagine yourself, this solitary and wretched being – who is willing to meet death with a smile – as the only relief to his anguished mind; and then you can form some idea of the writer's feelings when he bade, "adieu" to all he held dear on earth, and turned his back upon his Mother's home.

It was then, indeed, he felt; a stranger in his own land and as willing to die as to live. But the pangs of separation are, after a time, removed and the wanderer looks forward to the happy moment, when he will be again surrounded by his friends, and treading upon ground, every inch of which is endeared to him, by fond associations of childhood.

I find that I have been transgressing from a faithful posting of my Journal and have allowed my feelings to proceed my pen, scarcely knowing what I have written. And now as it is done, my friends must forgive me, if I occasionally allow my pen, to portray my feelings – – and wander from my original subject. And now once more to my Journal.

On the morning of the eighteenth of December I bade adieu to friends and home, and at an early hour in the morning, might have been seen winding my way toward the boat that was to carry me to my "Ocean Home".

On my way to the wharf, I tarried – at the residence of my friend, John McKaraher, who much to my delight intended accompanying me to New Castle, at which place our ship was awaiting the arrival of the Captain and myself. After taking leave of his family, (how often do I think of the last words I then heard pronounced; "Remember absent friends"), my friends John and William Magill, and myself proceeded to Race Street Wharf, where we found the Steam Boat Clifton, ready to carry us to New Castle, Delaware. There a goodly number of my friends had assembled to say "Good Bye" and load me with their good wishes. I was not permitted to enjoy their company long, for soon, the last bell sounded, which seemed to say; the hour has come, when you must tell that fatal word "farewell". 'Twas done, when it could no longer be avoided – and the boat was moving off in the stream.

I remained, riveted as it were, to the spot from whence I had last looked upon those I loved; until the spires of my boyhood's home, had recedeed from my view. My friend, John, proposed our descending to the Fore Cabin from which was issuing those sounds which 'tis said "doth soothe the savage ear" and as he remarked, will drive away dull care. It was then, a tear, stole to my eyes and trickled down my cheeks unbidden and unchecked. 'Twas then, I fancied a tear would be shed by those I left at home when they learn 'twas true that I had gone ––(Vain! vain mortal).

Upon entering the cabin we found the music to proceed from a violin, in the hands of a sailor who was accompanied by the others.
All were gloriously "in for it", as the saying is. The trio were dancing and singing; much to their own satisfaction, and greatly to the amusement of a large number of passengers, who had found their way to the Social Hall. These three sailors were intended for our vessel, in place of three who had run away from the Ship while lying at New Castle.

I thought, how different were the feelings of myself and these three sailors and of Capt. Watson, who was also aboard. He looked as happy and indifferent as the sailors, little, as if he had bid farewell to friends and home. He had become accustomed to it. The keener edge of his feelings, had long since been worn off by parting having been so oft repeated. Yet who can doubt that he did not feel a pang when parting with his family; when it was but four months before, that he reached his home, a shipwrecked mariner having lost his ship, while riding at Anchor, in fancied security at the Isle of Sol – – one of the Cape de Versa. But, sailor like he was, again anxious to be bounding o'er the briny deep.

We remained in the Cabin for some time, not, however, taking any part in its mirth and gaiety. We found company enough, in each other, and passed our <u>time</u> conversing of <u>times</u>, that were to memory dear; of friends whom every moment, separated still farther from me; and of course exchanged the usual instructions, upon the parting of friends; which all the world know are: To lose no opportunity to write and give all the news of the day. How often are such promises broken and treated as naught as soon as acquaintenances (not friends, for such they are not) are out of sight? It shall n'er be said of me that I forgot such a promise, or neglected writing to my friends. I know too well the value of a letter from home, when that dear place is far – far distant, to ever risk my not receiving those – "Shortner's of Distances" if I may be allowed so to call them – – by my own neglect and inattention during my absences. By close attention upon my part, I have better right to anticipate the same from others and when I return will know who are <u>friends.</u>

In a few hours after leaving the wharf we were summoned to dinner, and descended to the table to take our last meal together. I say last meal, yet I fondly hope it is not – yet many months must pass e'er we are again permitted to set at the same table and enjoy each others company. This meal was finished almost in silence, as regards we two friends. The time was drawing near when we must part, our hearts were full and both were wrapped in thoughts.———— Upon ascending to the deck, after dinner was finished, we observed that New Castle was open to our view; abreast of which our gallant Ship was now plainly visible, riding at anchor as if she were impatient to be bounding o'er the rough and boisterous sea.

In a few moments more we were landed at New Castle. Our luggage was hurried promiscuously from the boat to the wharf and then she dashed onward to her destined port of Salem.

A signal which we made before the boat left us, soon brought our ship's jolly boat to the wharf, by which we first shipped our three sailors and their luggage. Upon returning she took the baggage and sundries belonging to the Captain and myself; and the third time, Captain Watson and myself took our seat in the stern sheets. As I clasped the extended hand of my friend, John, and with tears in our eyes, we faltered out the words "Good Bye", the boat was pushed off from shore. The oars were feathered, and soon we were safely landed on the deck of the Roanoke, the boat which a few moments before; was floating gracefully o'er the smooth and placid waters of the Delaware, was now hoisted close up under the quarter and lashed fast, which seemed to say – "Now there is no escape."

The merry song of our sailors, as they hauled the anchor home, the quick and sonorous voice of our Pilot, as he gave his order; Man the wheel; lose the main topsail, fore top sail, brace forward the yards, and a host of others following each other in rapid succession was enough to convince the doubtful mind, that we were in deed under way. At three o'clock, with a fine breeze and all sail set, we were ploughing the waves of the good old Delaware, and riding proudly on towards the bottomless deep.

About nine in the evening, our Pilot thought it advisable to come to and anchor, and await the coming of the morn – – which was accordingly done, anchoring abreast the Brown; being then forty miles from the Capes. At an early hour, all was bustle and activity upon our deck; and long before the rays of the morning sun, had shone their lustre o'er the plains of Jersey, our gallant Ship was again underway, driving on under a full prep of sails. Captain Watson determined that our ship should not forfeit her laurels for fast sailing, as we were opposed by two fast sailing vessels, the Wm Brown and Walter, both like ourselves outward bound.

At eight bells, our Steward announced breakfast as being ready, which being famished, I seated myself to write Cape letters for home. With a heavy and throbbing heart, I applied myself to the task, as, although a pleasure, it was a task.

I had scarcely finished, when our Pilot obtruded his head in the companion way and accompanied it with, "Please close your letters Mr. Reynolds, as we are now abreast of the Cape, and shall leave in a few moments."

At half past twelve, a small skiff from the Pilot Boat came along side. Our Ship was laid too, and the Pilot, true to his word now left us, with pockets well filled with letters, and repeated injunctions to forward them immediately upon his reaching shore.

Now that our "Little brief Authority" had left us Capt. Watson, took command, and issued his orders, "Pull away the Main Yard." We were soon riding o'er the waves, like unto a thing of life, a true emblem of mankind, not knowing upon what rock or shoal, or at what moment, She would be lost or destroyed.

The day was cold and unpleasant, a very high sea running, and a keen searching north west wind; nevertheless, I deserted the Cabin as soon as my letters were closed, and remained on deck, until our pilot's boat was lost to my sight. Then, directing my eyes towards my dear native land, awaited patiently for the moment when it should be snatched from my view. For this I had not long to await; as the wind was fast wafting us from the land that gave us birth, and scarce three hours had passed after parting with our Pilot ere the heights of Hanlopen has disappeared from my sight; leaving naught to gaze upon but the vaulted sky above, and the roaring sea beneath.

It was in vain that I gazed in the direction of our vessel's wake, endeavouring to obtain still another last and lingering glimpse of the land of freedom; until the shades of night had drawn o'er us, leaving naught to be seen, save unbroken darkness. Not one of the many million stars, which usually bedeck the heavens, appeared to cheer and direct the mariner on his lonely way. All, all, was dark and dreary. All that was heard, was the heavy and measured tread of the watch, as he paced the deck, the groaning and crackling noise of the vessel, as if acknowledging the mighty powers which moved her, the grating of the rudder, the howling of the wind as it rattled through the rigging, the loud roar of the mighty billows as they broke with unrelenting fury o'er our vessel; and every half hour the dreary sounding bell on the Fore Castle, as it tolled forth, how fast the moments flew.

At such a moment, it was fit time for reflection, and soon after supper I retired to my berth. There to give free vent to my thoughts and feelings. Oh! How my heart reverted to my dear home, and those dear friends whose society I had been so used to enjoying. A thousand trivial incidents, long since past and forgot, now stole upon my mind and reflected with more than ten fold weight and strength, than they did at the time of occurrence. The long list of friends and acquaintances we hastily run o'er, and many who perhaps had not for months occupied a single thought in my bosom, were now brought vividly before my mind. All were then dear to me; and none were forgot. I felt a kind of melancholy pleasure in recalling to my memory those by-gone days of bliss and pleasure, happy hours which will never more return, those delightful scenes which my eyes may never more behold, those dear friends whose pleasure it was to have me with them, and administer to my many wants, and the many comforts of a dear "Mother" home. I repeat, that it was a melancholy pleasure to recall all these to my memory; and they impressed me with feelings which time will never cause me to forget. It was not until midnight had passed, that I had rest for my weary mind; when Morpheus threw his Mantle o'er me, and wrapt me in the sweet embrace of sleep.

Our cabin is of a very good size, but is very poorly lighted, whilst at Sea. It is necessary to close all the Dead Lights, and the only light then admitted, is through the Companion Way, which has a door opening on either side, with a descent of nine steps. There is a sliding window in front and one on each side, abaft the doors. The State rooms are four in number ; they are small and inconvenient. Two contain two berths each, and the others, one. They receive light from a "Bulls Eye", as they are called, which is a small glass, placed in the deck, immediately over the room, of about nine by two inches.

Such is the room which I expect to occupy for at least one half of the coming year. I doubt whether I shall ever be aroused by the rays of the morning sun penetrating to my berth. That it will be uncomfortable, when in warmer weather; I do not doubt. But as it is yet winter time, I find it very comfortable. When we get in to a milder climate, and fine weather; the dead lights will be again opened, and then it will be more pleasant.

We muster in all, fifteen souls, namely; Captain, First and Second officers, seven men, cook and steward, two boys, including Sail maker and Carpenter; the former called "Sails" and the latter "Chips", and myself. Our Ship is of 318 Tons, Register, 109 feet long, 25 feet Beam, and 18 feet Hole. A yellow streak is on her side; Scroll figure head, and mounts no guns. She has black Yards with a house on deck, covering the Companion Way and wheel, and having on each side State rooms to accommodate the 1st. and 2nd. Officers. Such is the "Ship Roanoke", and such is what I now claim as "My Ocean Home".

For several days after leaving our coast, we had a continuation of very heavy gales, accompanied with, rain, snow, and hail, and very cold weather. When we left the Capes our Bows were covered with ice, which formed while riding at Anchor off the Brown. It was a very high sea, running, and our vessel laboured continuously.

On the night of the twenty second Captain Watson and myself had just bade "good night", and were about retiring; when we were startled by a cry on deck of, "Oh, My God! The rudder is broke." In an instant we were both on deck, and found the bolts which secured the Wheel ropes, had drawn entirely out of the deck and had nearly killed two men, who were stationed at the wheel. The stove and the panels in the state rooms, on both sides, were bounding with frightful velocity, from side to side, the Ship entirely unmanageable, and it was blowing a perfect hurricane.

After much labouring and the united strength of the whole crew, the wheel was again secured, and by cutting through the State rooms, and bulwarks, and passing a rope around the stanchions, the wheel ropes were made fast, and the Ship, after an hour of anxiety and hard work, was again manageable, and brought to her course; unable, however, to carry any sails as the gale had increased to such strength.

The ship was laid too – – under one small sail, until about day light, at which time, it had moderated so much as to enable us to carry close reefed main and fore top sail.

For the last three days we have had very pleasant weather, and what is of far more importance to the mariner, than a clear sky — a fair wind.

I did not escape that much dreaded malady the "Sea Sickness"– – owing to the weather being so boisterous and the Sea so rough. For two or three days I was quite under the weather. It is useless to attempt to describe it, as those who have once experienced its sensations, know far better than I can tell them, what it is. Those who have not experienced it, never will know, until they have a trial of it. To say the least of it, it is an awful and wretched feeling, and may be called a "Contradiction". As you feel sick, and yet are not, or at least, cannot be. You feel at times, disposed to eat, yet the very sight or even the smell of victuals, disgusts you. There you lay – – too weak to stand upright, too cross to talk, and too sick to eat; in fact, you are completely helpless, and feel as willing to die as to live. But when once recovered, you find your appetite considerably improved, and feel disposed to eat all that can be placed before you. Such were my feelings and I suppose has been the same as with others.

Since leaving the Capes our course has been South East, and every day brings us to a milder and warmer climate. Vessels bound to South America from the United States are obliged to run, a great distance to the eastward, in order to prevent being set to the leeward of Cape St. Roque, which is the most easterly point of South America, lying about 35 degrees West Longitude. All navigators endeavor to cross the equator in from 20 degrees to 27 degrees West Longitude, and then the greatest caution is required to weather the cape, owing to there always being a current setting to the westward at the rate of about two to two and a half knots per hour. It will be observed, by reference to the map, that a passage from England to South America is equally as short, as from the United States.

We have had several sails in sight, and exchanged signal with one homeward bound. She was at too great a distance to enable us to speak to her. Since leaving, we have celebrated Christmas upon the broad Atlantic, and some of my friends, no doubt, wonder what <u>Ben</u> had for dinner, on that day. So to those I will say of what our <u>"Bill of Fare"</u> consisted. Firstly, a fine large roast turkey; secondly, roast beef, thirdly, corn beef, fourthly, boiled ham, turnips, onions, potatoes, mince pie, almonds, raisins - - and a glass of wine, to the health of "Absent Friends". Such was our Christmas dinner, and think would vie with many dinners which were served up on that day, upon the fast land- - both in point of variety and good cooking. And to add to the comforts of the day the weather had become so pleasant as to enable us to eat without having a fire in the cabin, and to allow one of our dead lights to be opened. Our steward, so far appears to be a very good fellow, and to understand his business. And as we have plenty of chickens and ducks, I think we shall at least have some <u>bones</u> to pick for a long time to come. We have still a fine turkey left, which is intended for our new year's dinner. Tomorrow being New Years- - a fine young porker will have his throat cut this afternoon; to furnish the crew and all hands <u>fresh</u> dinner, to commence the year with.

I should much like to spend tomorrow with my friends at home. It will be the first New Year's day I have ever passed, away from home, and heartless and unfeeling as some think me to be, I sincerely trust the next one, will find me in the bosom of my friends, and that will then and there find, that "Time" - - The changer of all earthly things, has left <u>them all unchanged</u> and that Death has been to all - - as a stranger.

CHAPTER TWO

January 31, 1840
Ship Roanoke, At Sea

As most practical bookkeepers rarely post their books, oftener than once a month, you will observe that I am following their example, and now once more resume my Journal, which is also my Blotter and Ledger, with my head for a day – book, for the purpose of posting it up to the present time.

One would suppose, that a person having so little to do, and so much leisure time, would post his acts every day. But if I opened my book daily would be considered, as altogether too minute an observer of small affairs, and as noting down every little action and expression, as I am compelled to write in the cabin, it being too – dark to accomplish it in my state room, even at mid–day. I do not mean to imply by this, that a person can be too minute an observer of light and trivial things; for it is from such that Man found his opinions, and from trifles that the character of men is often, too truly ascertained. Trifles light as air, and by themselves, as naught yet, when linked together, form a chain, which will resist a Giant's power, to break. The probability of being considered <u>personal</u> by those who are my daily associates, and perhaps the strongest and best reason, not having much to journalize that would interest the reader has been the cause of my not daily posting my Journal.

It can not be supposed that one would have much to communicate, which would be interesting, when shut out, as it were, from the whole world, with the same associates day after day; with naught but Ocean beneath.

The scene is always the same, yet ever changing. Today the sea will be aroused and raging with all the fury of an untamed lion, and tomorrow as calm and mild as the bleating lamb. At one time the heavens will appear resplendently clear, and the horizon, skirted with the ethereal rays of the glorious luminary, the Sun. Again 'twill be wrapt in darkness, and that which, a few moments before was beautifully clear, will now be fringed with clouds of the blackest hue, leaving naught to be seen of its former splendour and glory.

Occasionally the inhabitants of the mighty deep, will play about our vessel, and the birds flit on airy wings, and soar far o'er our tall tapering masts, away toward the skies. We have but to look around us and we see that "God is everywhere." To Nature's Student, no field presents a wider and more boundless scope, than the deep and mighty Sea. That which at first sight appears a useless waste of waters, is an indispensable provision of the Creator for our preservation and benefit. It renders communication more easy, with the countries it seemingly divides, and by flowing from warm to the cold regions, equalized in some degree the temperature of the earth, and the vapours, breezes and showers arising from it refresh and soften the earth, and contribute to the sustenance of beast and vegatation; as well as man, for the want of which, the whole earth would become as a desert, and mankind cease to exist.

Again I am wandering from a faithful performance of my task; so once more to the posting of my Journal.

I commence with "New Year's Day"– which although passed far away from friends and home I am compelled to say, was by far, the most pleasant one I ever have passed. I speak only, as regards the weather. It was the first I have ever passed, without a fire. Thermometer standing at 12 noon at 70 degrees – Windows and doors open, and all hands in complete summer dress.

As there were not many of us to exchange the usual good wishes of the season, we consoled ourselves by mixing a famous pitcher of Egg Nogg – – not made of milk, as is usual in all civilized countries; but water, and drank a "Happy new year and many returns" to those dear friends, from whom we were and still are, fast, hastening away.

Our dinner was very similar to that on Christmas, and I doubt whether those at home who spent more money than us, had one half the real enjoyment or relished their dinner more than we "poor sea tossed souls".

Nothing of particular moment or interest has occurred during the month. Every day has been but a repetition of the preceding one, with but little variation or change. When within four degrees of the Equator we had light winds and calms, which lasted for four or five days, during which time, we had a number of heavy showers, accompanied with much thunder and very vivid lightning. During the month we have passed ten Sails, all on the same tack as ourselves; so far nothing has passed us, save the winds – – which is quite as pleasant, as being passed by others.   When in 8 degrees North Latitude we spoke an English brig, bound for London, and desired to be reported by her twenty three days out from the Capes. On the 20th we crossed the Equatorial line and bade adieu to a northern for a southern line, being exactly thirty one days after discharging our pilot- - Eleven days of which we spent between 8 degrees North and the line.

The old custom of "Shaving" , all who cross the line for the first time, I believe, is now almost entirely done away with, on board merchant vessels, though still strictly adhered to in men of war. In former days all who visited the line, for the first time, were regularly "Shaved" by old Neptune or his self appointed deputies. On board of Dutch vessels it was usual for them to "Keel Haul", as it was termed, all green hands. This was done in the following manner. First; by squaring the Fore yard, attaching blocks to each yard arm, through which were passed ropes, having one end of each, made fast on deck, and the other two joined together and dropped over the bow of the vessel. To this rope they attached their subject, hanging weights to it to sink him, below the keel of the vessel. The rope was then manned on both sides, by the crew, the one side pulling whilst the other slacked; in this manner the poor fellow was literally keel hauled - popping up his head on the port and then on the starboard side of the vessel. So goes the story, for the truth of which I will not vouch, but for the credit of this civilized age, it must be said that nothing of the kind has of late years, been done.

In other vessels it was customary to place a quantity of water in the longboat, and when about the time old Nep or his agent generally appeared, and inquired if any of his children were on board, and on being told, in the affirmative, he invited them to a seat in the longboat, saying at the same time, "That he always liked to see his children carry a clean beard." Often he found it necessary to call in the assistance of some of the elder ones, in order to place the junior on the Barber's Bench. When once seated, Old Nep commenced his operation, and with mop brush, and slush or grease pot in hand he lays a thick coat of lather upon the face of his child. After which he produces his razor, which was generally a piece of old iron hoop, and if the patient was not of a very amiable disposition, the more uneven the surface of his razor, the better, as he then could give pressing marks of his affection. The shaving having been completed, the patient is at full liberty to make his exit as soon as possible, which he is not long, in doing, as all hands, ready to wash him as soon as Neptune, gives him free, and are at liberty to wet him as long as he continues on deck. When once clean, and his dress changed, he is at full liberty, and may then join the rest, and assist in washing the next subject.

Our vessel has been a scene of bustle and confusion during the whole month. To one who never made a sea voyage, it would be astonishing to witness the work that is generally going on, aboard of a ship, whilst in fine weather. Many suppose that when a fine wind follows a vessel, the crew have nothing else to do, but seat themselves and relate stories and tales. But it is not so, as they always have something to do, some rope wants mending, some part of the rigging requires to be repaired, or something else done. Our Sail Maker has been constantly employed in his vocation, and has already finished several new sails. Our crew have been busily employed, in preparing our vessel for the rough and boisterous regions of Cape Horn, to which we are now fast approaching. In fact all has been activity and not an idle moment has been spent by one of our crew.

On the 23rd we passed and spoke the Danish brig, Proven. Upon nearing her, the Captain hailed us in very broken English - "Ship Ahoy! Where was you from and where am you going? What was de Longitude and how long am you out?" To all of which questions, Capt. Watson respectively answered and asking in return where he was from, where bound, and how long out? He received for an answer, "From Gibraltar, bound for Rio de Janeiro – – <u>sixty five days</u> out." By this time we were leaving him rapidly, and there being no time for further conversation we bade him adieu, wishing him a safe and <u>speedy</u> passage and flattering ourselves that we were not aboard the dullest sailing vessel in the world; as we had sailed double the distance, and in half the time, that this poor fellow had. We were then sailing seven knots, and he only about four.

On the 25th, one of our crew, who was aloft engaged at work in the rigging, described a Sail ahead – which upon nearing, proved to be an English man of war brig. When abreast of us, a boat came off from her and was soon alongside, from which, a fine looking young man, of about 23 or 25 years of age, dressed in white duck pantaloons, blue cloth jacket, trimmed with gold lace and ornamented with buttons, bearing the English Crown, and with a cloth cap encircled with a broad band of gold lace; mounted our deck. With a slight inclination of his head, and touching his cap, bade us good day, accompanying it with, "I suppose you are from New York?" "No Sir." was the response of our Captain. "We are from Philadelphia." He was invited down to the cabin, where he seated himself, apparently as much at home, as if he had commenced the voyage with us. Although, he evidently endeavoured to be easy and agreeable in his address, there was that reserve and hautiness about him, which invariably characterizes an Englishman.

His vessel was the "Brig Partridge" of 18 Guns from Rio, bound to Pernambuco. They had been four months from England, cruising on the African and Brazilian Coast, in quest of Slavers, and had not heard from home since leaving. As we were plentifully supplied with papers we furnished him with some, containing our "last news from England" per Steam Ship, Liverpool – – which gave him news within sixty days from home, after having been carried over eight thousand miles and laid at home, fifteen days out of that time. So much for Steam Power.

He enquired if we had passed any Slavers, and was much pleased to learn, that we had passed a vessel, which was evidently a Slaver, only the day previous, bound towards the Brazilian Coast, and as she could not have been more than six or eight hours, astern of us, we will not be surprised to hear of her being captured. After taking the name, tonnage, etc. of our vessel, and a glass of wine, he took his departure, promising to report having boarded us, upon his arrival at Pernambuco, to which place they were bound for stores.

Fortunately I had prepared several letters for home, and had closed them, but four days previous, in order to be ready in case we fell in with any vessel homeward bound, and eagerly embraced this opportunity to forward them, via Pernambuco. Should there be any American vessels there, I anticipate their reception at home, about the first of April. During the month, we have had a great number of fish swimming near us, but although we made our best endeavour, were unable to catch any of them.

We have long since lost sight of the "North Star", but still the Mariner, who should chance to be without a compass, is not deprived of a mark to steer by in a Southern Sea. No sooner is the North Star lost to the sight, than the "Southern Cross" appears to view. This consists of four bright stars so situated, that if a line were to be drawn from one to the other, it would form a complete Cross, pointing towards the South Pole.

Whilst sailing in warm latitudes, the sea appears to be filled with a sort of animalcule or small animals, which are exceedingly luminous at night, and produce a beautiful phosphorescence on the waves. The path of a vessel is a line of light and the waters she throws up in her progress appears like liquid fire, myriads of luminous spots or stars float and dance upon the water and assume the most beautiful and fantastic appearance. The darker the night the more luminous and brilliant, they appear and present a most singular and interesting sight.

We are now past the limits of the "Trade Winds", so called from their constantly blowing within certain latitudes, for the same quarter, for the greater part of the year. Were it not for these winds, a passage across the ocean would be tedious and uncertain, but as they generally blow from the same quarter, a ship is enabled to sail for weeks without changing her course or disturbing her sails. Their limits are well known. A Mariner can calculate with some little certainty, as to the probable time required to make his voyage, according to the distance he expects to carry these Trade winds.

Our weather, is still pleasant, although the thermometer is gradually falling, as we progress to the South. We are now in twenty six South, with our days thirteen and a half hours long, and the Sun to the north of us – – and when I again open my Journal to post up the approaching month, we will have the temperature much cooler and the days still longer.

CHAPTER THREE

Ship Roanoke – At Sea
March 1, 1840

Again I find myself seated with pen and book in hand, for the purpose of posting my Journal for the past month. But for the past month, another thirty days have passed and gone and still I am sailing o'er the mighty deep and tossed about, at the mercy of the winds and waves.

This day, one year ago, I sailed from the Capes of the Delaware, bound to New Orleans, and took a last and lingering look at Cape Henlopen light house, as the sun retired to his ether bed, beneath the gilded line of the western horizon; little thinking then, that at this time, I would be riding on the bosom of the Pacific, ten thousand miles from home.

The past month we have experienced all kinds of weather. Fair and head winds, calms, rain, hail, and snow, and as regards nearing our destined haven have made but poor progress, when compared with the previous part of our voyage. We have had head winds, where generally at this season, the Mariner looks for fair weather. Becalmed for ten days, when off the River Plate, where nine tenths of the year, it blows a perfect gale; in fact it appeared as if the elements had combined against us, to prevent our progress to the South. We have sailed only about one half the distance, we did in the previous month; but such is the Mariner's luck, he is bound to all weather, and must make the best of whatever comes.

The commencement of the month, our Ship was a complete paint shop. We painted her entirely, fore and aft, inside, at which business I lent a hand, and with a few more attempts, think I might be able to handle a paint brush, with considerable skill.

During the time we were becalmed, the Sea was beautifully smooth, and as placid as the limped stream, which winds its silvery threads through the green deck and meadow; so much so that a stage was rigged outside of our Ship, and the vessel scraped and painted.

We have not met with a single sail, during this month, naught, but the sea birds and the fishy inhabitants of the briny deep. Since we reached the Latitude of 39, we have seen millions of birds, and of several different kinds, among which were the Cape hens, about the size of a half grown chicken, mostly of a brown colour. The Molineaux, which are about the size of a full grown duck, variegated in colour, with large bills, are shaped like the Eagles. These birds fly in immense flocks, and rest only during the calm; when hundreds of them are seen floating gracefully o'er the surface of the water often approaching within a few feet of the Ship. We have also seen a number of Albatross. These birds, when setting on the water, appear very similar to the swan, though they are often much larger, measuring from sixteen to twenty feet, when their wings are extended. The usual size of them is about five feet, and the largest we have seen, I should think would be about twelve feet across the wings.

On the 23rd our eyes were greeted with the ever pleasant sight of land, being the first we had seen since our departure; during a period of sixty-three days. It was Staten Land, a small island situated to the east of Terra del Fuego, and separated from the main land, by the Straits of Le Mare, which are about thirty in length, and vary in breadth from fifteen to thirty miles.

It presents a very barren and rugged appearance, high rocks and mountains, without the least signs of vegetation. Some of the peaks are covered with perpetual snow. We passed within four miles of the shore and as we were abreast of it, at the rising of the sun, it presented a beautiful appearance as the rays of the morning sun, shone directly upon the snow capped peaks and crags, giving them the appearance of being studded with diamonds. But when once deprived of the sun's rays, and at a greater distance from it, it has the appearance of an irregular map of dark blue clouds. With a fine breeze, we soon sailed round to the south of it, and lost sight of the land with the going down of the sun.

In this part of the world, it is generally blowing a gale of wind, and equally, rough and boisterous weather. It is considered by all, to be the most stormy part of the seas and fine weather is seldom or ever looked for. We have, thus far been much favoured, although we have had several heavy gales and for the last six days been sailing under close reefed sails, with a continuation of head winds, yet the gales have not been of long duration.

We have at last weathered Cape Horn, but been obliged to run as far as 59 degrees South Latitude and in a few days more our vessel's bow will be turned to the north, when we shall think of arriving at our journeys end.

A very melancholy occurrence which took place a few days since, has cast a gloom o'er the countenance of all. It was on the afternoon of the 25th, when the crew were called to reef top sails during a gale of wind. They had reefed the top sails and were then reefing the main sail when our carpenter, who was on the lee yard arm, in reaching over to fasten the "earring" as it is called, lost his balance and fell over the yard. He clung for a few moments to the earring, hanging as it were between heaven and earth, until naturally becoming completely exhausted, he gave a death shriek, and fell senseless into the raging sea beneath.

Ropes, chicken coops, spars, boards, etc. were in an instant, thrown within reach of him but he made not the least exertion to grasp them, and was hurried away with his back turned to the ship and ere the jolly boat could be cast a drift, he sank to rise no more.

I viewed it as a miraculous interposition of Providence, that the unfortunate victim sank so soon, as, had our boat left the vessels side, neither boat nor crew would ever have returned, as there was too high a sea running for the boat to have lived, and we should have had the loss of more than one to mourn. Every exertion that human power could make was made to save him but 'twas all in vain. He was called to the Bar of the Almighty, and no human hand could stay the summons. No tombstone worked by man marks the spot where his frail form reposes. The sea shells are his tombstone, the seaweed his winding sheet, and the coral rock his coffin. The bones and sinuous which once formed the man now mingle their dust with the clear flowing billow, and the keen winds as they play o'er the angry surge, sing his last sad dirge.

It is always customary when a shipmate is lost at sea, to make a vendue of his wardrobe, among the crew. The proceeds of which the law compels the owner of this ship to retain one year and one day– and if in that time, no relative of the deceased appears to claim it, it is paid over to the "Seamen's Society " for the relief of indigent sailors. According to custom, the following day, we had a vendue of the affects of our unfortunate and much lamented carpenter. The chest was carried to the quarter deck and opened in the presence of the crew. Our first officer acted as crier, and soon found ready sale for his entire stock.

Though a solemn and serious occasion one could not look on with out smiling to see the competition between several of the crew, for different articles. As an instance; a pair of old rusty razors brought $3.50, and a piece of brown soap of about three pounds weight, sold for forty eight cents. Why they run the price of this soap so high, I am at a loss to tell, as none of them appear as if they ever molested their skin with anything akin to it.

The complete wardrobe, chest and all other traps brought about forty dollars, which in these days, is a large amount for the effects of a Sailor, as the majority of them, come to sea with scarcely a third change to their backs.

Since leaving the Latitude of 26 degrees, we have experienced nightly, the dews, which are incident to a Southern atmosphere. They are perceptible at the moment of sun set and long before his rays have ceased to be deck the heavens. Everything that is in the least exposed, is as wet as if it had been raining, and for several hours after sunrise, the water is dropping off the rigging and Sails. Now we do not feel them as we have the wind from the south which is cold and dry – it being generally with the northerly and easterly winds that they are the most perceptible.

We have been gradually lowering the thermometer, as we progressed to the South and for the last week it has ranged from 52 degrees to 39 degrees, which I anticipate is as cold as we will have it during our passage. With the thermometer at

39 degrees and no fire to sit by, it is not an easy matter to keep warm unless one lay abed. It pinches pretty smart, and as our supply of wood, is short, and on allowance for cooking, we cannot enjoy a fire in the cabin. Consequently we are compelled to keep as comfortable, as we can, without it.

We are now out seventy days, and I must confess, I am quite sick of the monotony of ship board, and shall hail with joy the moment when I again set foot upon Terra Firma.

Our fresh stock is fast approaching to a close. Our chicks are reduced to four. All our ducks went over board, with the coop, which was thrown to save the Carpenter's life. And our <u>Gutter Snipe</u> are reduced to two, yet with care and a little economy, we hope they will last until we reach Valparaiso.

We are now moving rapidly to the Westward and I trust that ere another month has passed I will be able to announce to my friends at home, my safe arrival at our destined port, with the temperature somewhat warmer, and the weather much more pleasant; than it now is.

CHAPTER FOUR

At Sea
March 25, 1840

Once more I resume my pen, to post my book; contrary however to what I promised to do when first I commenced it, which you will remember was to post it, the first of every month. If I should leave it until then, I am fearful I would be obliged to finish my "Sea Account" after my arrival, which task I do assure you would not now be an unpleasant one, as I long to have my eyes once more greeted, by the sight of land; but yet, not with that throbbing heart, that I shall once more welcome the sea washed shores of my own dear home, should I conclude to return.

Since my last, we have made still slower progress towards our destined port than we have done in the same length of time since we left the placid waters of the Delaware. We have, however, weathered the most boisterous part of our passage – as Cape Horn is admitted, so to be, by all. Indeed there is no part of the world, where there is such a continuation of gales, squall, as are always to be encountered off the southern part of the western hemisphere. From the 28th of February to the 22nd of the present month, we have had a continuation of gales and storms; not squalls, but gale upon gale, each increasing in strength and length of duration.

For several days it was impossible to make any headway, without hazarding the safety of our Ship. Several times we have been obliged to heave-too, for twelve and twenty hours during the twenty four.

The most severe gale we experienced was on the 18th and 19th; during which time we were "laid-too", under Main Spencer and reefed Spanker, the latter was not long set, before it was blown to pieces – – and in place of it, a small sail was lashed, in the Mizzen rigging, which by laying against the shrouds, was supported, and withstood the fury of the winds. Before setting this sail, Capt. Watson placed his large oil-cloth coat in the rigging, but it was not sooner up, than the sleeves were blown from it, as if it had been but paper. It was with the greatest difficulty, that a man could ascend the shrouds, and then only by dragging himself by main force from ratline to ratline. A tremendous sea was running which was indeed awful to look upon, and the spray driving with such velocity that it had every appearance and cut as keenly, as if it had been hail.

But, thanks to an ever kind Providence, we weathered the gale, with the loss of only one spar, and a few of our head-boards; driving the whole time, the Sea was breaking o'er us in all its fury, and every moveable thing floating about the decks. Every spare rope was then brought into requisition, to make preventer braces, and strengthen our rigging. It was only owing to the most untiring exertion on the part of all hands, that we lost no more.

On the night of the 19th it had so far moderated as to enable us to carry close reefed top sails, and put the Ship off before the wind. Some idea may be formed of the severity of the gale when I mention that we afterwards found by observation that during the time we were "heave-too" we were driven, <u>dead to leeward,</u> the distance of sixty miles – – being about three knots per hour that the Ship was carried sideways.

On the third day the wind had greatly abated and the sea fallen considerably, and we were making fine headway, with a smooth Sea and fine settled weather, and gradually drawing a warmer climate. The temperature this morning being 58 degrees.

We are now within two hundred miles of Valparaiso, and expect to reach there in two more days time.

March 26th. – – This morning we have had our eyes greeted by the ever welcome sight of land. We have had it in sight since eight o'clock this morning, and find by observation, that we are now (12 o'clock), about forty miles from Point Corumilla, which is at the entrance of Valparaiso Bay.

The day is beautifully clear, though a very high sea running, and a strong head wind setting directly off from the land. The land appears to be naught but mountains beyond mountain, and far in the rear, the immense peaks of the snow capped Andes, are plainly visible, stretching their lofty summits far above the clouds, and as the sun is shinning on them in all his brilliancy, they present a beautiful and picturesque appearance.

Unless the wind should haul to some other quarter it will be impossible to enter the bay before tomorrow, and we will be obliged to lay "off and on" until daylight once more appears, and then I trust that ere another Sun has set, we will be safely moored in the harbour, after having performed this long and tedious voyage in safety.

Our ship is now a scene of bustle and activity. Some employed bending chains, others stripping off "chaffing gear"; others cleaning the brass work, and in fact all employed, dressing the vessel in her "Sunday or Harbour Suit". It reminds me of a lady, when equipped for a ball or party; she muffles up in an old cloak, old bonnet, old shoes, etc., and after arriving at her destined haven, she throws off, all the <u>old – covering</u>, and appears before the gazing company, in all her best attire; little resembling the decrepit old-woman, who entered the mansion a few moments before.

So it is with a ship, while on her passage, she is dressed in old clothes, but upon entering port, all the old garments, are thrown off, and she appears, like the lady in the ball room, dressed in her best attire, with her <u>stays</u> well taught and <u>all her rigging</u> well <u>braced</u>.

CHAPTER FIVE

Valparaiso
April 1, 1840

Again I open my book, and am most happy to record that I am safely landed on Terra Firma. As was anticipated, we reached port on the morning of the 28th of March, being then ninety seven days from Philadelphia, and having sailed in that time, according to our log, about twelve thousand miles.

The evening of the 27th, we ran within four miles of Point Commilla, situated near the entrance of the harbour. But owing to the weather being hazy and thick, and a very unfavourable wind for entering the bay, we were obliged to wear ship and stand off from shore. We were to await the coming of the morn and at first dawn of day we again stood in for port; it blowing a gale of wind, and our gallant little ship under close reefs.

Judge of our chagrin and disappointment when Captain Watson, after taking a lunar observation, announced the fact of our being twenty miles to leeward of the port, and that unless the wind hauled, it would be impossible to reach an anchorage that day.

Whether Captain Watson thought, a second time, or not, I am not prepared to say, but to us it was – at eight bells, although the wind had not abated in the least, he gave orders, to turn out the reefs, and added in the same breath – "Look out for wet jackets, for what she will not do over the water, she must do under it." The reefs were soon shook out, the sails hoisted home, and our vessel pitching and driving, throwing the water fore and aft, and rolling her lee gunwale under-water. The water was flying over her at such a rate that it was impossible to remain on deck and escape being completely saturated. This driving, we were much pleased to observe, had the desired effect of drawing us to windward, and at ten o'clock, we had the satisfaction to open the port directly ahead of us. In another hour we entered the harbour and were completely surrounded by small boats, well freighted with live stock from shore.

As soon as the visit of the Custom house and Port officers were passed, our decks were covered with people of all ages, condition, and sizes. They came tumbling over the sides of our vessel, and lit on the decks like so many black birds upon a cornfield, each endeavouring to be the first one aboard to receive all the news and retail it out to his more dilatory companions. Then followed the same set of questions from one and all – – where from, what cargo, to whom consigned, how many days passage, what news? etc.,etc., and several enquired "Have you brought any letters for me?" Supposing of course, that we never would have left home, without knowing such a celebrated and consequential personage as Me, Me.

Among our many visitors I found one, from the house with whom I expected to transact my business; and who politely offered me a seat in his boat, and to conduct me to the counting room.

As I was already dressed and had my papers in my pocket, and having answered the numerous questions of our visitors, I accepted the offer of my newly made acquaintance, and took my leave of the ship. The moment she was brought to anchor, and after a pull of about a quarter of a mile I landed on the Mole of Valparaiso. We took a short, though very rough walk, through a narrow crooked street, which brought me to the place of business of my consignees, to whom I delivered my letters. As a matter of course, I answered numerous questions, and went through the usual forms that a stranger does upon his first arrival.

The only circumstance that occurred to damp my spirit, and settle disappointment on my brow, was the fact of being answered in the negative when I enquired – if they had letters for me! The answer I received was the most distant from my thoughts, as I confidently anticipated that letters would have reached here before me, by way of Panama. But, the answer was "No, for you have brought the latest dates by at least sixty days."

There I remained until five o'clock, when a servant entered the counting-room and announced dinner as being ready. At this hour the store is closed and all business for the day, suspended. The store and dwelling are both under one roof, the building is two stories high. The upper part occupied as the dwelling and the lower story for the store. There the merchants and their clerk reside, enjoying the same comforts, eating at the same table, and all; as it should be everywhere else, on terms of equality and familiarity. Not so, is it in our country for how often it is, that clerks are treated, more as hirelings, than companions. – But to dinner – We (Captain W. and myself) were ushered up to the dining apartment; a fine large room with three windows opening to a verandah or piazza in front. In the centre of the room stood the table, well supplied with all the varieties of the season, to which about twelve of us sat down. The dinner was brought on in six courses – the first, was soup, then followed in succession, fish, beef, poultry, vegetables, etc., pastry, and fruit which consisted of peaches, pears, apples, figs, grapes, etc., and last of all coffee was handed round; this I think a decided improvement and observe it is customary and they never consider the dinner finished without it.

After setting at table for upwards of two hours, the movement was made to adjourn, and we all retired to the parlour, which is situated at the extreme end of the building, and commands a beautiful view of the whole harbour. There we remained until eight o'clock at which time a cup of tea and toast was handed round and finished the meals for the day.

Our host regretted his not having a bed to offer us, as their house was full – and as it was growing late. Capt. W. and myself, took our leave, and started in quest of lodgings for the night; as we could not return to our ship, there being no shore boat allowed to leave the Mole after sun–down.

We applied for quarters at the principal hotel, but found they were all full; yet as a particular favour, the landlady of the house, offered to have beds made for us in her setting room. As we were not disposed to seek lodgings elsewhere, for fear of not being successful, we readily accepted her offer and while our beds were preparing we took a stroll through the town, and returned almost blinded by dust, about eleven o'clock, We were then shown to our room in which were the two beds. One made on a sofa, and the other on six chairs – into which we soon tumbled, Capt. W. taking the chairs and myself the sofa. In a few minutes we were wrapped in the embrace of sleep, and so ended our first trip ashore.

At six the next morning we arose, and returned to the ship, to take breakfast, after which we came on shore and attended to our business of the day.

Not liking the appearance of the hotel, where I spent my first night, I looked for other quarters, and succeeded in finding a very quaint house, kept by an English lady, with about ten boarders, where I expect to remain during my stay in Valparaiso. It is said to be a well kept and cleanly house, when compared with others in the place, but according to my notions of cleanliness, it has nothing to boast of. I lodge and take breakfast here but always dine with some one of the gentlemen whose acquaintance I have made or to whom I have carried introductory letters by all of whom I have been treated with the greatest kindness and attention.

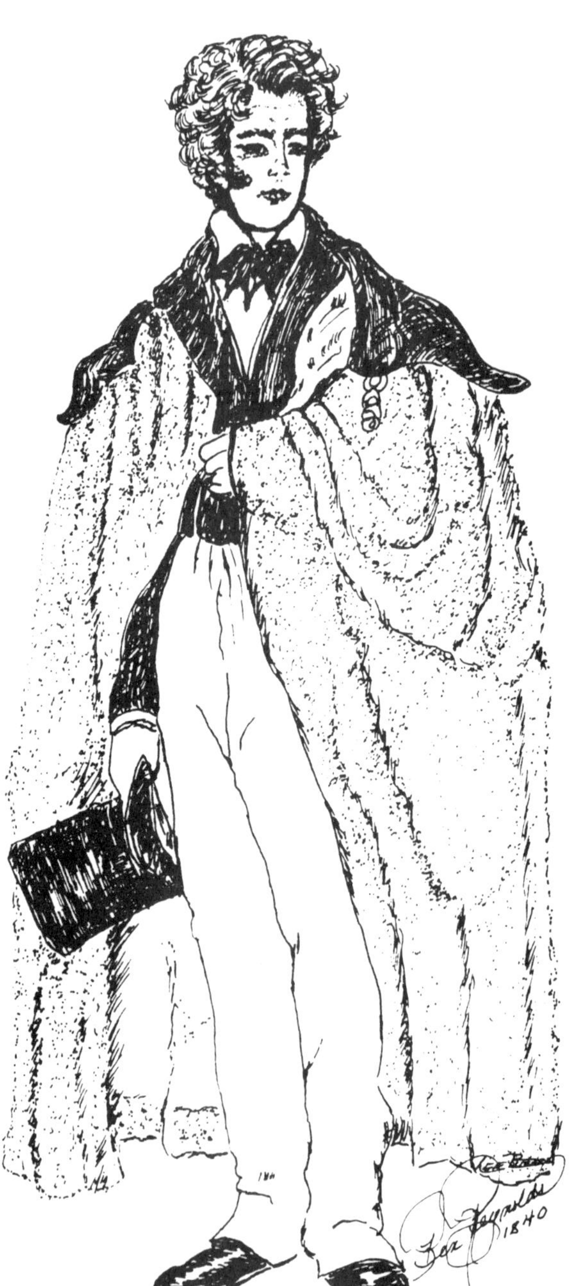
1840

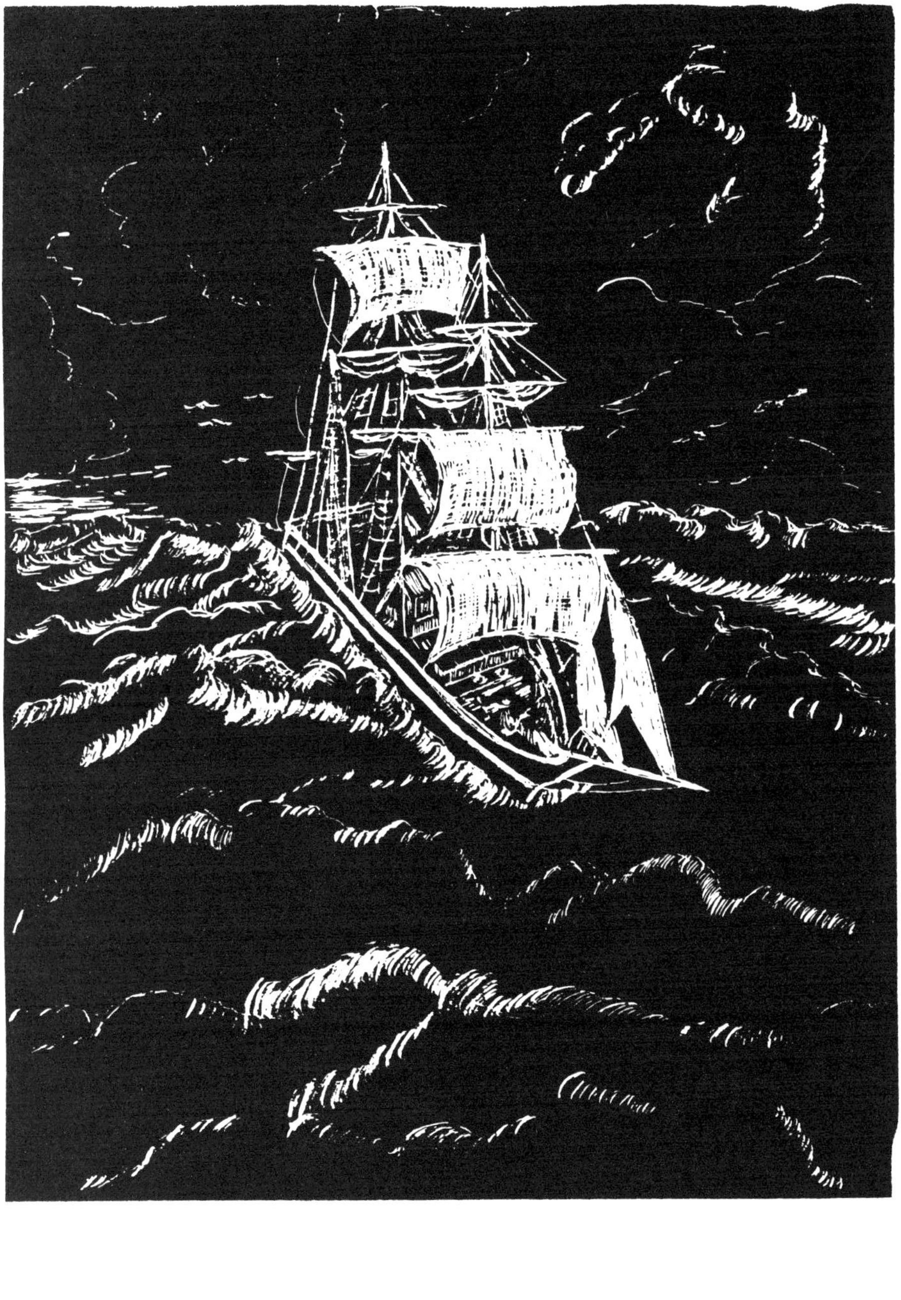

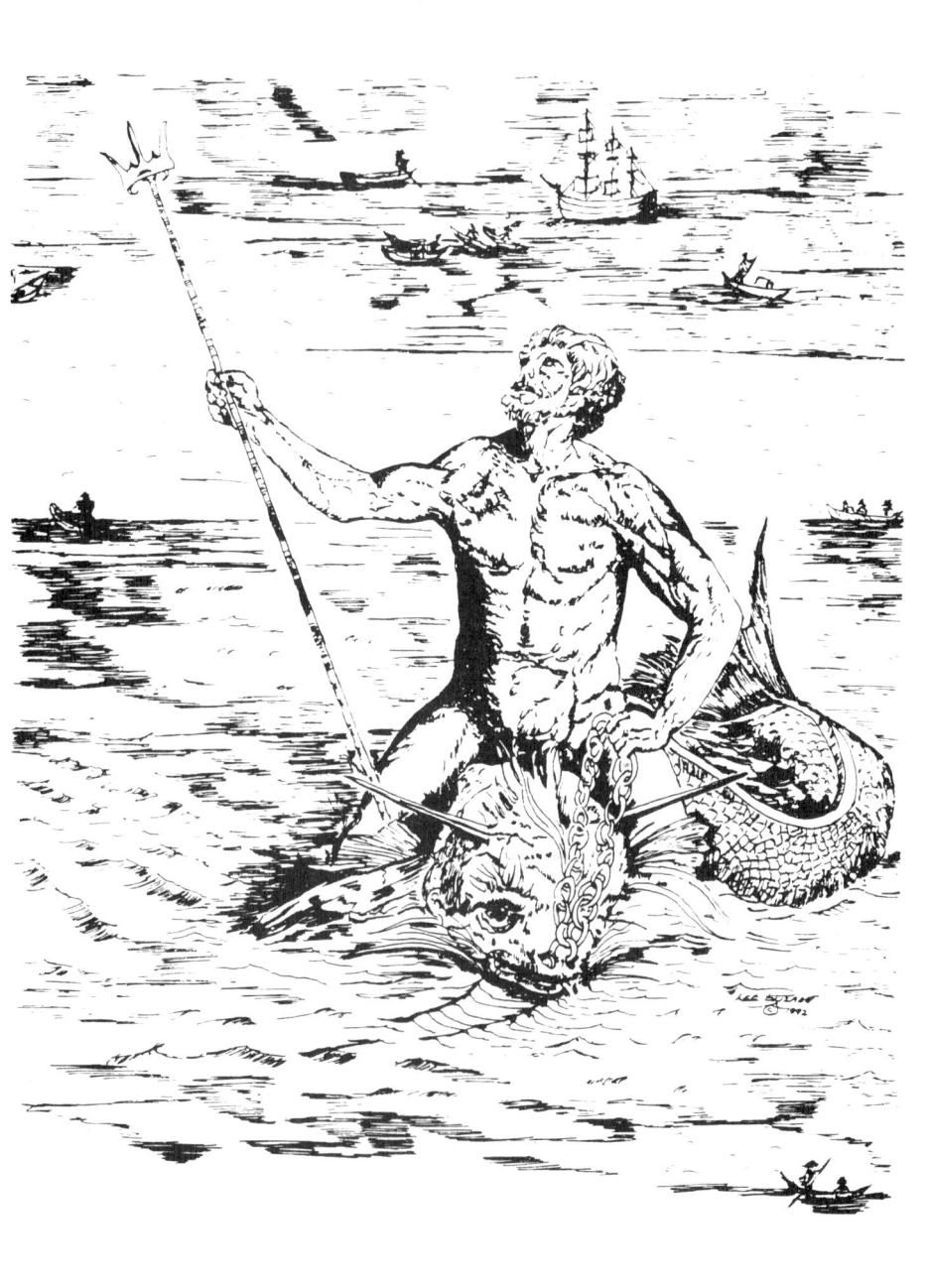

SEA VOYAGE
of
BENJ REYNOLDS
1840

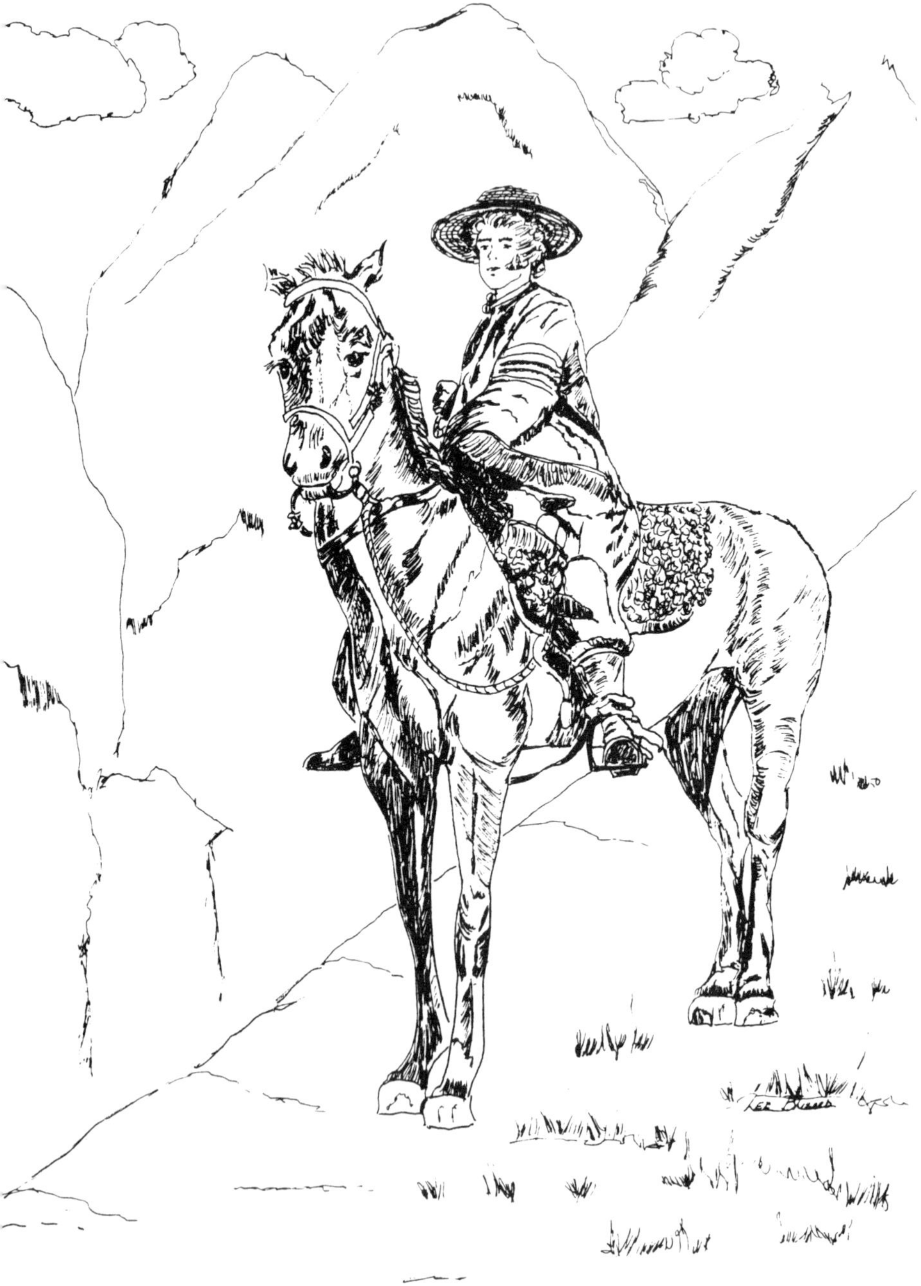

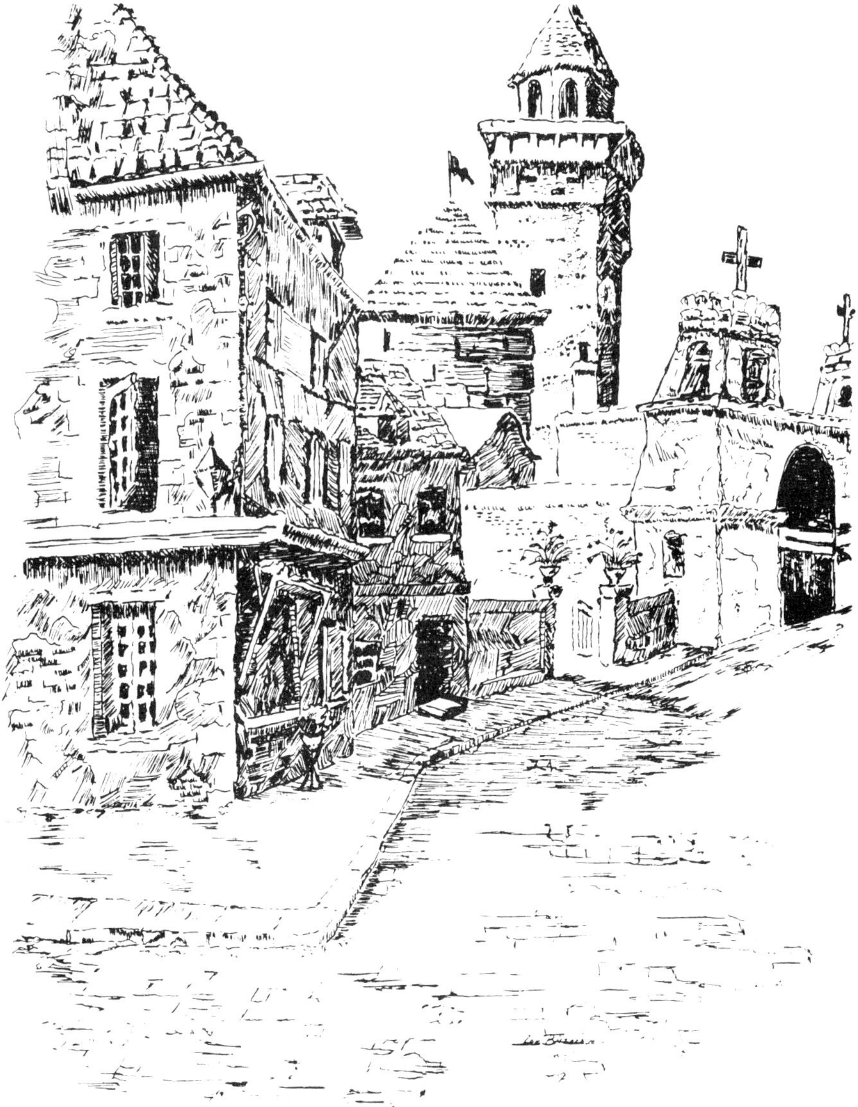

CHAPTER SIX

Valparaiso
April, 1840

I suppose my friends will not admit, that I have fulfilled my promise, unless I make some mention of the port of Valparaiso. So I will attempt a description of the place by commencing with it's harbour, Valparaiso Bay, which forms nearly a semi–circle, opening to the northward, and about fifteen miles from the east to the western most point. It is surrounded on all sides by lofty hills, varying in height from one to three hundred feet, immediately back of which rise another range averaging about one thousand feet. They rise abruptly, almost from the water's edge, particularly to the southward, and about half form a kind of recess, and the hills are not so perpendicular. The harbour is defended by a fort, situated on the eastern most point, and an old battery, on the west side, under the guns of which the U.S. Frigate Essex, Commander Porter; was captured by the British Frigate Phoebe and Sloop of war Cherub, after a desperate and gallant resistance of two hours and a half – on the 28th of March, 1814.

The harbour would accommodate two hundred sail of vessel with safety, most of the year. But not during the prevalence of the northerly winds, which blow with great violence from June to September – at this time not more than half the number could lay with safety to each other. At this season of the year the harbour is a dangerous and unsafe one – as vessels are apt to drag their anchors, and be driven ashore, which is the case almost yearly, and often attended with loss of life.

Directly before the town, within fifty yards of the dwellings, on account of its proximity to the sea, a tremendous swell sets in during the prevalence of the northerly winds.

The trade of the place has greatly increased within the last ten years. In 1810 the only vessels visiting it were from Lima. In 1822, they had forty one national vessels, and in 1829, thirteen foreign vessels entered and left and now the flags of most commercial nations may be seen in the harbour at all times floating at the gaffs of fifty to eighty sail of vessels. Always several Men of War, English and French, and occasionally a <u>Strolling American</u> touches here, but seldom longer than to get supplies. Shame, Shame, to our Government. The only vessels we now have on the coast, are the Constitution and St. Louis – and Commodore Clarkson has announced his intention of making Talcuhuana his head quarters, which is a small port to the southward of Valparaiso, at which no American vessel ever stops, except our whalers, who enter for supplies and to refit.

The city, or as it is called, the port of Valparaiso, is built principally in the Quebradas or valleys and upon the hills which surround them. The stores and business part of the town are built with their backs directly on the water's edge, so close that in many places the surf breaks upon them. The street is long and irregular, following the winding of the shore and in extreme length– about one mile and a half.

Most buildings occupied as stores, are two stories high, the upper part occupied as dwellings with verandahs or piazzas front and back. The remainder, as I have before mentioned, are built in the valleys, and scattered about the hills without any regard to streets or uniformity of appearance. They rise from the base to the summit of the hills, one above the other, so that two thirds of the inhabitants can set in their parlour and look over their neighbor's roof. The houses are mostly built of mud, one story high, and all white– washed, which with their red tile roofs and irregular situations present a novel and interesting appearance upon entering the harbour.

It contained in 1822, a population of 10,000, and now it is said to contain about 35,000 inhabitants, one seventh of which number are foreigners.

It can boast of no fine buildings, though the Custom House and Church of Santa Domingo are large and good buildings. They are built of bricks, made of mud and straw dried in the sun, and are rough cast, with the walls about three feet thick, in order to prevent being shook down by earthquakes.

It contains no manufacturing of any kind, and depends entirely upon foreign countries for supplies. It carries on a considerable coasting trade, and as all goods are received and shipped from the Mole directly in front of the Custom House, it presents a scene of great bustle and activity. The inhabitants are mostly of a light brown or malay colour, varying however, according to their situation in life. The lower class, which constitutes the greater part of the population, are of a much darker shade than the higher and more respectable class of inhabitants – who by inter–marrying with Europeans have become quite white or of a very light brunette.

The females are generally stouter and shorter than the ladies of our own country, and unlike most others on this coast, are not afraid to show their face, and may be seen at all times walking through the street, or enjoying the cool and refreshing sea breeze, upon the beach. They seldom or ever wear bonnets, but have their hair very neatly dressed, generally plain in front with two or three and sometimes four plats hanging down their backs. If there should be much dust flying, they raise their shawl over their heads, which protects their hair from the dust as well as their heads from the sun, as they seldom carry parasols and never appear without large shawls.

The greater part of the men are poor, uneducated beings, mostly in the employ of the merchants, and known under the name of peons. All merchandise is carried by these peons, lighters loaded and discharged by them, and all goods carried to and from the custom house. It gives employment to a great number. They are generally stout, athletic men, and capable of lifting immense weights, from their constant practice and being accustomed to it from their childhood.

They form societies of from fifty to one hundred, each paying a fixed sum out of his earnings, into the funds of the society, which is appropriated to the support of their sick, and to pay for any goods they may damage, while loading or discharging the lighters, as they are obliged to wade into the water, up to their middle before reaching the boats.

The markets of Valparaiso are well supplied with beef, mutton, veal, poultry of all kinds, vegetables and fruit of all descriptions; now through the winter season you may find in great abundance, peaches, pears, apples, figs, grapes, etc. – – all of which can be purchased at very reasonable prices. The only necessary of life, of which the inhabitants are deprived, is a plentiful supply of fresh water, as there are no springs or wells in the town, and all the water is brought from neighbouring springs and small riverlets, in skins or casks, and carried on mules. Some is carried five or six miles. Fire wood is also very scarce and commands a great price. It is brought the distance of twenty and forty miles, loaded on mules – with some fifty or more in a drove.

The regulations of the police, are excellent, and cannot fail to elicit the admiration of all foreigners, and make him feel assured of safety, where so much order and regulation is observed. They may be seen at all times, day and night, at their post of duty ever ready to protect their laws, and guard the peaceable citizen from the lawless ruffian, or midnight assassin. The officers of the day are all mounted, wearing short swords, and pistols, and known by the name of Vigilante (pronounced ve–he–lanti); they are all provided with whistles, and should they have occasion for assistance, all that is necessary is to sound them, which is returned by others who follow the sound, and in a few moments they have sufficient force, to enable them to perform their duty. Those of the night are the same as our watchmen and are called Sereno; they are armed the same as the vigilante, and generally have a Spanish cloak thrown carelessly over their shoulders to protect them from the heavy dews which nightly fall. These Serens cry the time every half hour, and sound their shrill whistle which is responded to from all parts of the town, and should any person be walking in the streets after eleven o'clock, they whistle him the moment he passes, so he is passed from one to the other and a good look out kept, to see where he brings up. By this vigilance, many robberies are prevented. But should any be detected in house breaking or stealing, they are punished with great severity, generally confined to prison for three or five years, obliged to work on the roads in irons, and publicly whipped, every two or three weeks, a certain number of times according to the pleasure of the judge. This whipping is performed first before the place the robbery was committed, and then on the Mole, that being the most public place in the town.

When a gang of convicts are brought out of prison, to repair the street on roads; they place a guard over each man, who is responsible for his return to prison, and should he be allowed to escape , the soldier is obliged to serve in his place; so it may be conjectured that the convict is not allowed to move far without guards.

The prevailing religion is Roman Catholic, and four churches of this order are built in the port. They are quite common place buildings, and very plain when compared with the churches of other catholic countries, (this from hear-say).

As the sun retires to rest, on his ether bed, beneath the gilded curtain of a western horizon; the silvery sounding vesper bell, calls upon all true worshippers, and tells them, 'tis time for prayer; then, countless numbers of the inhabitants may be seen winding their way through the many paths and passes of the hills, towards the building which bear the proud insignia of the "Holy Church", and beneath which so many thousands adore, there to prostrate themselves at the foot of the Holy Cross, and perform their devotions as becomes their profession and faith. The day preceding good Friday, stores were ordered to be closed and all business suspended until Saturday morning at ten o'clock.

During this time no one is allowed to enter the port, and after three o'clock on Thursday no person is allowed to leave it, and no riding through the port is admitted.

Among foreigners this is looked upon as a general holiday and most of them visit the country during their continuance. As I was a foreigner, of course I must do as foreigners did, and accordingly I accompanied three gentlemen, a distance of twenty miles to a renshaw, or mud cottage, owned by one of them, for the purpose of gunning and recreation during the holidays. At three on Thursday we were prepared to start – mounted, booted, spurred, and equipped in true Chilanian style; with our chilano saddle, formed of a number of goat skins, called pallons, strapped over a wooden frame and which are the most comfortable saddles a man can possibly ride; and ponchos and leggings, to protect us from dust, and broad brimmed straw hats, to protect our heads and face from the sun. Thus equipped, we started on our journey, and after a pleasant ride over the hills, and from our high elevation, having the port and harbour in view most of the time, we arrived at the renshaw about seven. We dismounted, not the least fatigued by our ride, though with a very good appetite for supper.

The renshaw is built of mud, one story high, about forty feet long by twelve wide. It is divided into four apartments, neatly white- washed inside and out, and covered in with a well thatched roof, formed of small reeds. It stands on the side of a hill, at the foot of which lies the rich pasturing valley of Con-con, hemmed in on all sides by high and lofty mountains; through the centre of which a small stream bearing the same name, winds its serpentine course, rushing with great rapidity over rocks and sand banks, until it looses itself in the broad Pacific, three miles distant. A luxuriant and well trained grapevine winds its innumerable arms o'er a rude arbour, which extends the whole length of the cottage, and affords a fine shade to the front – through which the searching rays of the loving moon, finds it impossible to enter, and is obliged to leave all beneath in unbroken darkness.

The silence which reigned here, unbroken, save the rushing of the waters of the river, and the loud roar of the mighty deep as it broke on the rocky and iron bound shore, three miles distant, the reflection of the moons silvery rays upon the bosom of the turbulent stream, and the sparkling sound on its boarders, the cloudless arch o'er head, which seemed to rest on the blackened brow of the surrounding mountains; bedecked with its countless millions of brightest gems, the broken and picturesque appearance of the surrounding country, the romantic situation of the renshaw, and the rustling of the leaves as they obeyed the impulse of the passing breeze all tended to give an air of enchantment to the scene, and is required but little working of fancy, for the beholder to imagine himself gazing upon one of the oft praised and bewitching scenes of far-famed Italy – – where all around is beautiful and serene, and description is but mockery.

Upon entering the building the visitor is struck with the neat and comfortable appearance. The first room contains a large side-board, well filled with crockery ware, knives, forks, spoons, glasses, etc. In the centre of the room stands a large oaken table, and on each side a red lounge, large enough to be used as beds in case of necessity. Leaving this room, you enter a smaller one, well filled with old bottles, dishes, etc., and used as a depository of trappings of their horses. Leaving this, you enter successively two larger chambers, each containing three swinging cots, bureau, wash stand, basin, pitcher, etc., in fact the house is provided with every necessary for house keeping as well as guns and fishing tackle, for sport and pastime.

Our first thoughts, after arriving were for supper, so after seeing our horses ungeared, saddles put away etc. – we proceeded to search the secret recesses of our saddle bags, as we were yet without the knowledge of their contents. After emptying them out on the table, we cautiously opened the several packages, and found that the majo–domo(head steward), had given us bread, butter, salt, pepper, cold roast beef, mutton chops, all ready for the gridiron, and several bottles of wine.

As we all had a remarkably good appetite, we concluded to have a warm supper, and sent for an old man, who lived near by and who attended to all visitors, to come and act as cook. The old man obeyed the summons and after an hours delay, served up our chop steak, very nicely cooked, and a pitcher of boiling water to make tea with. With these and the trimmings we had brought, we were enabled to make a hearty supper, and do ample justice to the chops and cooking of our newly appointed cuisinier. Supper being finished and dishes washed, we gave him free, with order to return in the morning with some eggs and young chickens for our morning meal. We then locked up house and started to visit a neighboring party of gentlemen who, like ourselves, had turned rusticks, and taken up their abode in a mud cabin.

When we reached their renshaw, we found to our surprise a party of twelve, all in high spirits, and engaged in the <u>innocent</u> amusement of playing cards. Here we remained an hour or two, accepted an invitation to join a ball party on the following morn and returned to our quarters after having had the dogs set on us for sounding an old cracked vesper bell, hung in the crotch of an old tree, which stood near the roadside. We escaped, however, without any damage and arrived safely as the renshaw, turned into our cots and soon forgot the pleasures of the day. At an early hour of the morning we were awakened by a loud rap at the door, which proved to be the old cook, who, true to his promise, had executed our order of the previous night, and was then waiting to obtain the gridiron, in order to prepare the chickens for breakfast. By the time we were dressed, beds made, and room put in order, we were summoned to breakfast. It consisted of four young chickens very nicely broiled, mutton chops, cold roast beef, boiled eggs, bread, butter, tea and coffee, – all these might have been found on the table, previous to our being seated, but whether we had a voracious appetite, or any part of our meal was removed by m... ic, I am not prepared to say, by true it was, that, when we arose from table, there was as strong proof in the way of empty dishes, as any host need desire, to satisfy him that his visitors were well pleased with the table he had set before them. This meal being finished to our entire satisfaction, we shouldered our guns and strolled through the country in search of game, climbing hills, jumping gullies, working our way through thick cane brakes, coming in contact with nettles, and getting entangled in briars, and firing away to the right and left – – but without the least success. It appeared as if the birds had a charmed life, as it was impossible for us to kill any, and we were obliged to return, as we had started, with our game bag empty, though much fatigued after a long and laborious walk, and perfectly satisfied with our gunning excursion among the mountains and valleys of Chile.

We reached the renshaw about noon, stretched ourselves on the bench, beneath the shady grapevine, and slept until a messenger arrived, to remind us of an engagement to join the ball party. So off we started and met them on the summit of an adjoining hill, where the ball was kept in motion until near dark, and then returned to quarters. We partook of a late dinner and amused ourselves the remainder of the day without moving outside of the house.

At an early hour, we turned into our cots, and despite the noise of the rats, and sharp biting of the fleas, soon forgot the toils of the day and resigned ourselves to sleep.

Long before the break of day, we closed our hospitable mansion, mounted our horses, bade adieu to the old chilanian, the romantic scenery of Con–con, and retraced our steps to the port, where we arrived after a ride of three hours, and just in time to change dress, and be ready for breakfast.

Our ride was indeed a delightful one, and fraught with truly grand and magnificent scenery. Our road lay over the mountains, at one minute two thousand feet above the level of the sea, and the next moment descending to the valleys. We were hemmed in on all sides by, apparently perpendicular hills, while far in the back ground and towering to the skies, the noble form of the lofty Andes rose in all their grandeur. In the midst of this, an ever burning volcano shone forth in all its splendour, contrasting strangely with the snow capped summits above, and the dark heavy appearance of the clouds, as they rested in detailed masses beneath.

The clearness of the sky, the purity of the morning air, the green appearance of the surrounding hills, our ever changing views, and the hundreds of mules laden with wood, water, fruit, vegetables, etc., with which the whole line of the road was filled, was all so entirely different from anything I had ever before witnessed, that it made a deep impression on my mind, and several times I unconciously checked the reins of my horse, and was lost in wonder and admiration while surveying the noble works of nature with which I was surrounded.

At ten o'clock several guns were fired from the Castello, which announced the holy days as being over, and gave permission to the inhabitants to renew their business, when the stores were again opened and the port resumed its usual bustle and activity.

I have already remarked that most of the houses are built of mud. The manner of building is as follows. A wood frame is first set up, then the interstices are filled with small reed, or brush wood, and over all a thick plaster of mud, with the ceiling and interim apartments of wood. This is the manner of building the better kind of houses, but with the more inferior, and by far the greater number, not near so much pains are taken, and if they have any pretensions to ceiling, it is generally composed of domestic muslin stretched from side to side, with cords in the centre, the same as a tent, to lower or raise it as a pleasure.

The Merchant's Exchange is a very neat and by far the best looking building in the place. It is two stories high, the first floor being occupied as an engine house, which are the remains of two old New York engines; the upper story contains the reading apartment which is a fine room. It is seventy five long by twenty five wide, receiving light from two large glass domes, placed at equal distances in the roof, and the extreme end which forms a semi–circle contains six large sliding windows, commanding a fine and un–interrupted view of the whole harbour.

The room is furnished with sofas, arranged along the sides, between each of which stand small mahogany tables, well supplied with papers and magazines from all parts of the world.

The walls are neatly white washed and on the sides are hung several valuable paintings. The windows are dressed with curtains of rich crimson damask, and the whole kept in good order. It is built by the foreign merchants of the port, and supported by their yearly contributions.

The inhabitants are very patriotic and have a strong attachment to their country. In order to keep these patriotic feelings alive in the bosoms; the national band, composed of some fifty or sixty musicians, are paraded through the streets every Wednesday and Saturday night, performing their national and most celebrated airs, and generally spending an hour in the plaza (square). All the inhabitants of the town may be seen flocking to the plaza, and the stranger is stunned with the oft repeated shouts, of viva Chile, viva Presidente, viva libertae, etc., which ascends from the mouth of men, women, and children.

All the men capable of bearing arms are enrolled in companies, the same as our militia; and the different divisions exercised every Sunday and paraded through the town.

The Plaza is a plot of ground which terminates the main street, of about two hundred feet square, neatly paved with small stones arranged in diamonds and squares. In this square several hundred women are mightily assembled, with large round baskets, in which they expose for sale all kinds of merchandise, such as boots, shoes, shawls, combs, plates, knives, cakes, etc. They arrange themselves in rows, each provided with a low stool to set on, and attached to their basket, a small staff about two feet in length, on which they suspend their lights, which are rude lanterns made of tin and glass, enclosing a huge tallow candle. The regularity of their arrangement, the great numbers of lights, the endless variety of goods they expose for sale, give the plaza an interesting appearance. The number of acquaintances one is sure to meet, makes it quite a fashionable resort for both, young and old. The women who attend here are poor, miserable beings, mostly Indians or half-breeds, and if anyone possess a stock worth eight or twelve dollars, she is considered rich, and as doing a great trade.

The climate is one of the most pleasant in the world. The thermometer seldom rising in summer above 85 degrees, or falling in the winter season below 60 degrees. The only inconvenience the inhabitants experience, is the long continued drought, and for eight months in the year they never have rain. During the whole of this time, from August to May, it is always clear sunshine, and a cloudy day is seldom or ever seen. But during the winter months, June, July, and August, they have a continuation of very heavy showers. Then the hills and valleys which have become completely dried up, by the scorching rays of an eight month's sun, assume a green and lively appearance, vegetation of all kinds flourishes luxuriantly. The hills become covered with wild flowers and aromatic plants of all descriptions and hue, among which the myrtle and cactus are very abundant and attain a great size. The most delicate plants flourish and bloom in the open air during the whole season.

Frost is not known, and snow never seen, except on the mountain tops, ninety miles distant, which can be seen with the naked eye during the whole year.

The products of Chile are wheat, barley, maize, tobacco, and copper, gold, and silver, one of which great quantities are annually obtained and sold to a foreign market, but there can be no doubt, but that many treasures yet remain undiscovered, as there has never been a regular and minute geological survey of the country and perhaps never will be, unless the people become more enlightened and intelligent, or it falls into better hands.

The usual mode of traveling is on horseback, and everything is transported on mules, as it is almost impossible to travel any distance with a vehicle, the country being so rugged and mountainous. A few gigs however are made use of between Valparaiso and St. Jago, the capital, a distance of one hundred miles, though it is attended with great risk, as the whole road is over mountains, in many places so narrow as barely to admit a passage for the wheels, while frightful precipices of three to four thousand feet yawn beneath you. The manner of traveling with these gigs, and their idea of resting the horses is curious and perfectly original and well deserves a passing notice. You start with one horse harnessed to the gig, a guide riding your side, whose horse is also attached to the vehicle by means of a strap, and a drove of eight or ten horses running ahead. When the horse attached to the gig, or those of the guide becomes fatigued, he rides ahead with his lasso, secures two others and exchanges them for those already fatigued. In this manner you keep changing horses, always driving the fatigued ones ahead, until you arrive at your journey's end, with all the horses you started with. This is their mode of resting horses, and it must be remembered, they go on full run, up hill or down is all the same to them, and should the gig be likely to upset or roll over a precipice, the guide gets out a knife, and cuts adrift immediately, leaving the passenger and gig to their fate. Horses are so numerous and cheap, that they do not value their lives, a good one not costing more than 20 to 25 dollars.

I should consider myself an ungrateful wretch if I left here without acknowledging the great and <u>marked</u> attention I have received from a numerous body of the inhabitants. Their politeness and kindness is only exceeded by their attention. They have been my constant companions, and so kind that I find it impossible to move without them. Wherever I am, there they are also, and it really appears that they fear to desert me for a moment, thinking they will not leave me sufficiently impressed with their boundless hospitality. But I do assure them, such constant though slippery friends, will, by me be long remembered, and the deep <u>impressions</u> they have left me with will ne'er be forgot. They are a regular body of <u>suckers</u> and are well versed in the art of phlebotomy. I shall herald their names far and wide, and make them known to all friends of mine who visit here. They constitute a great portion of the inhabitants, confine themselves to no one particular circle, but move in all societies. They are attentive to rich and poor, possess <u>strong attachments</u>, and though they visit without invitation and intrude where their company is not desired, they seldom require a second notice to retire. No sooner is a move made towards them, than they jump for some sly corner and there remain until the anger of their host has subsided. The affectionate part of the community are known by the very short, though expressive appellation of FLEAS. Do not start gentle reader and allow a chill of horror to convulse your frame or offend your delicate refined feelings, at the mention of that odious and detestable word, flea. For I do assure you "custom is everything", and were you here and see them as numerous as flies among douc'es of a confectioner on a mid summer day, you would consider one quite as common as the other. As regarded your feeling of delicacy as perfectly synonymous, particularly when you learn, that it is considered a great mark of gallantry for a gentleman to remove a flea from a lady whenever he may be so unfortunate to observe one, and that many, for fear of not having an opportunity, carry dead fleas in their pockets, in order to deceive the lady. They pretend to remove them from her person; and initiate themselves thereby, into her good graces of the fairer sex.

Owing to the volcanic formation of the country, earthquakes are frequent throughout the whole of Chile. None, however, have been very destructive for the last few years. The last severe shock was about six years since at which time one half the City of Conception was destroyed and a number of lives lost. Slight shocks are quite common, every two weeks or so and often more frequent, as has been the case since I arrived, in which time five shocks have been felt. Two of which were very heavy, but caused no material damage, further than shaking the loose whitewash from the walls, and rolling the detached dirt down the hills.

The shock was but momentary and was preceded by a loud rumbling noise, like that of a carriage over a rough pavement, though much heavier. Houses trembled as if they had been made of paste board, and the windows shook violently, in many places, breaking the glass.

Such a country may please some people, but I prefer a residence where the ground appears more solid, and the fleas do not bite so hard.

CHAPTER SEVEN

Valparaiso
May 1, 1840

The time is drawing nigh when I must bid adieu to the shores of Chile, and sail once more for the colder region of Cape Horn. During my stay here I have passed a delightful and pleasant time, and it affords me much pleasure, to acknowledge, before closing my book, the hospitality and polite attention I have received from all with whom I have had the honour to become acquainted. Nothing has been left undone that would tend to make my stay agreeable, and long will my visit to Valparaiso be remembered with feelings of gratefulness and pleasure, for the kindness and attention I have met with from one and all.

CHAPTER EIGHT

At Sea
June 12, 1840

Again upon the deep blue sea, and pitching o'er the briny waters of the great Atlantic- - To compel my friends to peruse another, "Sea Account" would be too great a tax upon their valuable time, as one account will answer for all, unless a daily log is kept, and it matters but little to them, to be told what winds we have, what sail we carried, or how many dishes are broke. So, I will run hastily over the present voyage, merely by giving the outlines, and promising to tax your patience but a few minutes.

On the afternoon of the 5th of May, the anchors of the "Roanoke" were once more hoisted home, her sails loosed to the wind, and a few minutes before sunset a gentle breeze wafted our gallant ship out of the harbour of Valparaiso. We have now an entire new crew. The old crew having run away during our stay in port. We also number more in the cabin than during our outward passage, having three passengers - - two French gentlemen and a Bolivian boy about ten years old. These gentlemen have been living in Bolivia for the last twelve years, and are now returning to their country via Rio, taking with them upwards of one hundred and thirty thousand dollars, being only a part of the fortune they have amassed during that time. The child is an adopted son and they take him to France to be educated.

Owing to adverse winds we were obliged to run to the westward after leaving port and on the third day out we passed in sight of the celebrated island of Juan

Fernandez, known by all children as being the residence of Robinson Crusoe, and in the afternoon the smaller one of Mas Fuerta, about sixty miles distant, which I suppose the author of Robinson Crusoe, fixed upon as the residence of Friday, previous to his visit to Juan Fernandez, and capture by Crusoe.

The island is rugged and mountainous, and can be seen fifty miles distant. It is the Siberia of Chile (though of more genial temperature than Siberia) to which they banish their convicts. The smaller one of Mas Fuerta has the appearance of one huge mound of earth, about fifteen hundred feet high, two miles wide, and five long. It is uninhabited at present, though a year or two ago it could boast of a population of one who belonged to one of the first families of Chile and was banished to the island for a pretended conspiracy.

We were obliged to run as far as 93 degrees west longitude before we could work to the south. There we got a slant of wind and run for Cape Horn, which we made on the twentieth day out. Our passage to the Cape was a continuation of unpleasant weather, raining almost every day and during the twenty days not seeing the sun one whole day. Though with all this, it was by far more pleasant than our outward passage, particularly as we had a stove in the cabin and plenty of wood. The winds being more steady and gales less frequent. It being winter season, we had the days but seven and a half and eight hours long from sun to sun, which seemed to rise and set nearly in the same place, we being eighty six degrees to the south of it.

We passed within twelve miles of the Cape with fine settled weather and studding sails set below and aloft.

The most southern land consists of a number of small islands, all bearing evident marks of having been formed by some powerful eruption of nature. The most of them are high ragged mountains, with their summits covered with perpetual snow, and the base presenting an irregular mass of sharp cragged rocks, without the least signs of vegetation, while far back on the main land of Terra del Fuego, a long chain of mountains, stretch their conical and heavy heads far above the clouds, on which the foot of man has n'er encroached, and where winter, clothed in his robes of perpetual snow, reigns in undisputed right throughout the year.

After leaving the Cape we had a renewal of head winds which set us to the Eastward of the Falkner Islands, and on the first of June, our summer (as I am still a northerner) was ushered in with a snow storm. The coldest weather we have experienced was off the Cape, when the thermometer stood at 40 degrees above zero. We soon ran into a warmer temperature as well as increased the length of the days and it is a pleasure to know, that we have weathered the most boisterous and stormy part of our voyage, and that every day brings us into fine and more settled weather.

During the passage we have not fell in with a single sail. We have seen a great number of birds and fish, such as porpoise, grampers, and whales. Of the latter we have had several fine views, they have been spouting on all sides of us, and in one instance a venerable looking old fellow about seventy feet long came close to our side with a young one not more than six feet in length swimming before her eye, we had a fine view of her, and were perfectly satisfied that she came no closer as a blow from the monstrous tail would have injured us considerably. When they are seen approaching too near a ship, the pumps are immediately manned, and the unpleasant effluvia arising from the bilge water offends their delicate nostrils, and they instantly beat a retreat, not at all pleased with their reception.

We have made several attempts to catch a porpoise, but without success. Once we struck a large one, which broke the harpoon and made his escape, thereby spoiling all sport with that instrument for the remainder of our passage.

We have just caught a large shark, being the first fish we have taken since leaving home. He measures nine feet from the "top of the nose to the end of his tail", and now has possession of the quarter deck, where he lays weltering in his blood. He offered so great a resistance, that four men were necessary to draw him from the water. We are now moving at a rapid rate with a fair wind and within a few days sail of port.

CHAPTER NINE

Rio de Janerio
June, 1840

We have at last reached our destined haven and, as will be observed by the heading above, I am again safely moored on Terra Firma.

On the morning of the 17th our ears were greeted by the pleasant cry of "land" and in a few hours we were in full view of the evergreen mountains and valleys, which on all sides surround the "Elysium of the South".

A gentle breeze wafted us towards the harbour and at mid-day we had the pleasure to pass the entrance and anchor a mile up the bay. Here we were obliged to remain and receive visits from the different boats of government. First came the Health boat, then the Palace, Port, and Custom House boats. By the time these visits were passed it was near sun-down. Then our jolly boat was manned, and the three passengers, Capt. W. and myself took our departure for the old city of St. Sebastian. After a pull of two miles, we landed on the mole of Rio, exactly forty-two days since our departure from the West Coast.

The mole, where we landed, was covered with people, (this I have since observed is a fashionable resort) where many of the inhabitants repair after the labors of the day, to enjoy the cool refreshing breeze and view the magnificent scenery of the harbour.

The moment I landed, a gentleman stepped up and enquired if my name was Reynolds and upon answering in the affirmative I received the pleasant information that he had letters for me. I of course accompanied him to his place of business, but found to my great disappointment that the letters were locked up in the desk of one of the partners, who had gone out to his country seat and would not return until the next morning. Consequently I was obliged to await his arrival before I could possibly receive my letters.

After taking tea with Messrs. W. W. & Co. I was piloted to a hotel directly opposite the mole where I had landed a few hours before. Here I took up my quarters for the night, and at an early hour retired to bed, (which by the by, was a sofa, all the genuine beds being occupied) and soon resigned myself to the arms of Morpheus, and the incessant boring of mosquitoes.

After passing a very restless and uncomfortable night, I arose at the first dawn of day and retraced my steps of the previous night, to the house of my consignees, took breakfast with them, and at ten o'clock had the satisfaction of receiving several packages of letters from home. With a trembling hand and throbbing heart I grasped the several parcels, stripped off the many envelopes, and for a few moments satisfied myself by reading the different hand writings, as I scarcely knew where to begin and felt completely lost among the rich treasures that lay before me.

After recovering from my revery, and suppressing the many thoughts with which my confused brain was filled, I proceeded to open and arrange these precious remembrances, according to their different dates. This done, I commenced perusing them with a throbbing heart, and it was with grateful feelings I learned that all were enjoying good health, and was pleased to have before me the precious proof that absent Ben had not been by all, forgot.

My friends will expect me, as a matter of course, to say something of Rio, and what I have here seen. But what can I relate which has not oft been told before, what would repay one for reading or myself for writing. However as my book still contains a number of blank pages I cannot well offer the excuse of want of paper, yet I feel before I commence how utterly incapable I am of doing the least justice to Rio and its beauties, by any attempt at description, with my weak and untutored pen.

In the commencement I am lost amid the beauties of its harbour, so justly praised by all who have ever entered it, and enjoyed the rich and truly magnificent sights which the eye meets on every side. Stretching inward as it does for thirty miles, and over looked on all sides by high and lofty mountains, its equal cannot be found in the world for truly picturesque and romantic scenery.

The entrance is a mile wide; on one side of which is the remarkable Sugar Loaf Mountains with a base of one mile, rising fourteen hundred feet almost perpendicular, and from its great height, giving the coconut trees on its summit the appearance of small shrubs. Opposite at the base of a huge mass of granite rocks, stands the fort of Santa Cruz, as impregnable as the rock on which it reposes on all sides with width of from three to five miles. On the eastern side a little below the city is the beautiful village of Rio Grande, with its neat white cottages standing in lively contrast with green hills which surround it. A little below and connected with the main land by a wooden bridge, passing between two high peaks of rocks a small island about a hundred feet high, attracts the attention of the stranger. On its summit stands an old dilapidated stone building, almost obscured by the coconut and palm trees, and dense foliage that surround it, which was erected by the Jesuits and formerly used as a nunnery, but now tenantless; and left to decay in all its solitary and romantic grandeur, a crumbling monument of those despotic days when the word of a "Pope", was law. All sorts of vice and villany were screened under the garb of religion.

On the opposite and immediately below the city the picturesque "Gloria Hill" rises in all its beauty, covered with the neat villa of the nobility, and their parks and groves of ever green foliage. In fact, on every side some interesting scene attracts the eye and one is lost amidst the multiplicity of prominent and truly magnificent views. The bay is studded with a number of small islands which like all that meets the eye is clothed in summer's richest robes. Two opposite and one below the city contain strong fortifications to protect the harbour from the encroachment of an invading power; and those farther up the bay are covered with country seats and rich plantations.

The shipping is scattered about the harbour to a great extent; those loading and discharging having different births assigned them, as well as the coasting and foreign vessels. Opposite the lower part of the city is appropriated to the vessels of war, those floating representations of the proud nations of the world, which are at all times to be found here.

Several hundred sail are constantly in the habour, but so great is its extent, they appear as naught, as all the ships of the world may be safely moored in the Bay of Rio, and still leave room for as many more.

The city of Rio de Janeiro is situated on the western side of the bay, about three miles beyond the entrance, and covers an extent of upwards of two miles square. There are several landing places for boats, but all vessels are loaded and discharged by lighters, which deliver their cargo, directly into larger store houses, built on the edge of the water, and may be in fact called "large covered wharves", as two thirds of the building stands on piles, with the water beneath it.

The houses are all built of stone, two, three and four stories high. The streets cross at right angles and are generally narrow, which with the height of the buildings, tends to protect them from the extreme heat of the sun, and renders the streets much cooler. They are barely wide enough to admit two carriages passing without encroaching upon the sidewalk.

The "Broadway" of Rio is the "Rue d'Ouvidor" in which the greatest number of fancy stores are situated. They are kept mostly by the French, who have the principal retail trade of the place. Their stores are arranged with great taste and present a very neat appearance, particularly the milliners and tailors, who have numerous imitation heads and busts, which they dress off in the latest fashion, and place in the most conspicuous part of their store, so they can truly say, though they have not always customers in their stores, they have at all times plenty of faces before their counters. The stores all have granite fronts and but few windows, being mostly doors, which are kept open during the whole year.

The city is said to contain 200,000 inhabitants. One half of whom are blacks and at least one third of the remainder are French, English, German, etc. so that not more than 66,000 are natives or Portuguese.

It contains a number of fine large buildings among which the churches must rank first. They are very numerous, all built of granite with steeples on towers, and surmounted with a gilded cross. The interior of them are very richly decorated, having a great deal of gilt work, numerous images of Saints, and dressed in crimson drapery trimmed with gold and silver lace. They are well supplied with bells which are rung without the least attention to con–cord, and produce a most discordant noise, when sounded for vespers, at the going down of the sun.

The Exchange, Museum, two Theatres and Palaces are fine buildings. The palace is a large commodious building, two stories high, about forty feet front by two hundred deep – is built of stone and rough cast, with a tile roof, like all the other buildings in the city. It stands back from the water about one hundred feet, having the ground in front as well as on the north side for the same extent, entirely open, and paths of flagstones, crossing it in all directions. The building is seldom occupied by the Royal family, as they remain at the Castle of Don Pedro, about three miles from the city.

The city is supplied with water, by means of aqueducts, leading from the neighboring mountains, into numerous fountains placed in different parts of the city – from whence it is carried by slaves to the dwellings.

The markets are held in open squares around the precincts of the city and attended altogether by slaves, who bring the produce in large open baskets. They are poorly supplies with meat and vegetables, but fruit of all kinds in the greatest abundance such as oranges, lemons, pine apples, bread fruit, bananas, tamarind, apples, etc. which is sold for almost nothing and constitutes the chief provision for a great mass of people.

Most of the merchants reside in the country, a distance of, from three to ten miles, riding into the city in the morning and returning about sun–down. The whole country is one complete garden. The houses are very neatly built. The grounds arranged with great taste and planted with monumental trees of all description. They are enclosed by low hedge with a fine stone gateway, on the sides of which lamps are hung. The grounds are filled with orange and lemon trees, palm, camphor, bread fruit, tamarind, embisella, coconut, and the umbrageous mango tree, through whose dense foliage even the sun's searching rays dare not penetrate. Also an endless variety of plants such as rose bushes, myrtle, jasmine, cactus, tulips, lady slippers, pinks, etc. — and to render the scene still more enchanting, a few have beautiful fountains, which throw their silvery stream into the pure white marble basin beneath. The whole appearance is beautiful and picturesque in the true sense of the word and (though I have never beheld them) I think would well compare with the so oft praised gardens of the East; as there is nothing that my imagination could fancy, would be more truly grand and beautiful than the rich scenery of the "Elysium of the South".

I last night visited the theatre, and had the pleasure to see the royal family, who were accompanied with all the ministers of state, the ladies of honour etc. The box appropriated to their use is situated in the centre of the house directly opposite the stage. It is highly decorated with gold and tinsel work in abundance, and screened from the audience by a rich suite of crimson silk curtains. It communicates with several rooms in the rear, to which the occupants retire during the interval between the acts. A few minutes before the commencement of the play, the curtains of the royal box were drawn aside and disclosed to view all who graced its seats. In the front sat the emperour, Don Pedro II – having on his left the two princesses and on his right the regent, who at present governs Brazil, and the chief minister of state. Back of these were the ladies of honour, the different ministers of government and attendants.

The emperour is a paleface youth, fifteen years old, rather stout with light hair and blue eyes. He was dressed in blue, with no other ornament than a few pieces of party coloured ribbon on his breast, and the national buttons on his coat. The princesses were dressed in rich figured satin, with short sleeves, white kid gloves, and earrings of the richest diamonds.

The younger princess is tall and slim, with a pale face and sparkling bright eyes. She walks very erect, is very animated and considered quite a beauty, altogether she "looks her title" if I may be allowed to express myself. The elder one is rather short and a little inclined to round shoulders, with a dull looking eye, unmeaning countenance, quite a common looking personage, and not to be compared with her sister. Of their relative mental qualities I can not speak but, if there exits as great a difference, as in outward appearance, then I should say that one of them, was merely a royal pet without any mental embellishments.

The house was filled from pit to gallery and from every quarter the diamond eyes of the Brazilian and French ladies shone forth in all their bewitching lustre, charming us poor mortals of the harsher sex as does the serpent his prey, with the beauties and dazzling brightness, which encompassed us on all sides, and riveted our attention in what ever direction we turned.

The play was performed by French amateurs who acquitted themselves remarkably well and entertained the audience until near midnight, at which time the royal family and suite took their departure in the carriages of state, drawn by six and four horses and the phaetons of the ladies of honour and attendants by two. They moved off to the sound of music accompanied by a mounted guard, and outsiders behind each vehicle, carrying in their hands large flambeaux to light them on their midnight way.

CHAPTER TEN

Rio ——July ——1840

I must not neglect to mention the hospital of Rio, known by the name of "Miserecordia". This is a large three story stone building covering about two acres of ground. One part is appropriated to the sick, another to the insane, another to the residence of the different keepers and a large portion to foundlings.

Directly opposite the miserecordia is the "Foundling House" in the front wall of which is placed a machine in the shape of a large lantern, with a small door in the side of it turned towards the street and a bell attached to it. The foundling is placed in this box which is immediately turned about into the inside of the building. The person who conveys the child rings the bell and leaves it there, upon which the proper officer comes and receives it without further esquires. The parent or friend who carried the child there generally leaves a note with it, declaring whether it be yet christened, the name it should be called by or the particular marks upon it. Here the child is nourished and provided for until it becomes five or six years old when it is removed. The boys are sent to the military school to be educated for soldiers, and the girls are placed in the miserecordia, where they are retained until a marriageable age. This building is open once a year for public inspection at which time these girls are to be seen, and anyone in want of a wife is at liberty to choose one from their number, provided the managers are satisfied that he is able to support a wife. If the girl is pleased with the looks of her suitor and accepts this offer, the marriage ceremony is at once performed and the wife receives a dowery from the hands of the emperour. It often happens that these natural children are acknowledged by their parents, and left heirs to large estates.

The annual visit of the royal family to the miserecordia took place a few days since. At an early hour, the streets leading to it were strewed with green leaves, and the windows of all the houses hung with rich drapery of all kinds and colour, and filled with the fair faces of the inhabitants and their friends, all arrayed in their silks, satins, and jewelry, and many holding in their hands bouquets of sweet flowers.

About mid-day the carriages of state arrived in the city. The first contained Don Pedro, sisters, and the Regent, and was drawn by six small horses richly caparisoned, then came the ladies of honour in the carriage of the princess, drawn by four horses. After them, the principal officers of government; the whole attended by a bodyguard and full band music.

As they passed through the street, flowers and wreaths were showered upon them from all sides, and wherever they turned they met with acclamations and expression of loyalty from thousands of their subjects, with whom the streets were lined. Upon arriving at the miserecordia, they alighted, and passed through the line formed by several companies of soldiers, to the church which occupies the centre of the building.

Here they attended high mass, and then the Emperour proceeded to lay a corner stone for an addition to this, already immense building.

The stone, containing the history of the building, names of those who officiated etc. was carried by the Emperour, surrounded by his ministers in full uniform, preceded by head bishop dressed in his robes of office, and crowned with the mitre, richly set with rubies and precious stones and trimmed with gold, and three old padres carrying his trail in the rear. Preceding these were carried several Holy banners. The Bible, Cross, Silver candlesticks, incense bowl, etc., the whole surrounded by padres carrying long wax candles, and attended by a body of soldiers.

The corner stone was to be laid in the ground which formed the yard of the building, and was enclosed by a large stone wall. The procession moved from the church around the outside the building to the entrance of the yard, a distance of about two hundred feet. The spot where the corner stone was to be placed, was enclosed by a low board fence, and surrounded by a crude floor strewed with green leaves. In the centre of this a small pulpit was erected, covered with crimson velvet and trimmed with silver lace and at each side a small stand covered with the same material. On these were placed the Crucifix, Bible, Candlesticks, etc.

Previous to the laying of the stone, service was performed, and then the conclusion of the ceremony announced by the firing of rockets, which were placed in all parts of the yard and attended by some of the padres.

The service being finished and corner stone laid, the procession retracted its steps, amid showers of rockets, and surrounded by thousands of people.

After this the Emperour and Princesses proceeded through the miserscordia, visiting the different parts of the building according to the annual custom. Whether he had an opportunity to bestow a dowery on any of the inmates of the foundling apartment, I am unable to say, as I was anxious to wait upon my dinner and did not remain until he had reached their part of the building.

The firing of rockets is quite a common practice among the inhabitants of Rio, and during their many holy days constitutes one of their principal amusements. During the evening fireworks, rockets and paper balloons are set off from all parts of the city and give the whole atmosphere the appearance of being filled with shooting meteors, playing about in all directions. In whatever direction one turns he is sure to meet with fireworks of some description or other and at the same time, the slaves amusing themselves by burning common fire crackers. Between the masters and their slaves you stand a fair chance to have your eyes put out, while passing through the streets during any of their gala nights. If this were allowed with us, we should soon see the city of brotherly love, reduced to a heap of smoldering ashes, but here, owing to all the buildings having tile rooves, there is no danger of their being set on fire, and they may burn powder, with perfect impunity and build bonfires wherever they please as there is no law to prevent it, and if there were, no police to see it executed.

As I have been obliged to be absent from my country during the annual celebration of our Declaration of Independence, it is pleasing that I have been permitted to pass the day in port and as an American am proud to record that I was present during the celebration of the 4th of July – – by the American Squadron lying in the harbour of Rio de Janeiro. The squadron on their station consisted of but two vessels and the sloop of war, Decatur, bearing the broad pennant of Commodore Ridgley and the Schooner Enterprise. The frigate Potomac has been anxiously looked for during the past months but there were no signs of her appearance until the morning of the third when an American frigate was signalized as being "off the bar". This set all on the tip toe of expectation; spy glasses were then in great requisition, and the entrance of the bay closely watched by many an anxious eye. Owing to light and head winds the vessel was not able to enter the harbour until after dark and then it was announced that the long looked for Potomac had actually arrived.

The morning of the 4th was ushered in with all the beauties of a clear and serene day. The first glimmer of Aurora disclosed to view the noble frigate safely moored in the harbour of Rio and riding at anchor in all her majesty and grandeur.

The day was beautifully clear, not a breath of wind appeared to be moving for fear of disturbing the serenity of the scene. The sun shone forth in all his brightness, reflecting his resplendent rays o'er the placid and silvery waters of the bay, giving the appearance of one vast mirror; interrupted only by the dark forms of the many vessels. The occasional passing of a lateen propelled by the brawny arms of their many slaves, or the momentary shadow of some sea bird floating o'er the harbour proclaiming its independence by it's short discorded notes which were soon lost amid the merry song of the swarthy slaves as they plied their numerous oars, o'er the unruffled surface of the waters. Nature appeared to have put forth her best exertions and left nothing undone on her part that would add to the charms or enjoyment of the day.

At eight o'clock a signal gun was fired from the frigate and at the same moment the glorious Stars and Stripes unfolded at the mast heads of the Potomac, Decatur, and Enterprise. About nine the frigate saluted the flagship with the "good old thirteen" which was returned by the Decatur gun for gun. Eleven was the hour appointed for the broad pennant of Commodore Ridgley to be hoisted on board the Potomac. At this hour, the Commodore, accompanied by his aid, took his departure from the mole in a neat gig pulled by eight hardy looking tars. The pennant was floating at the bow and the Stars and Stripes at the stern, waving o'er a pure white awning which was stretched o'er the boat to protect them from the scorching rays of a midday sun.

The frigate lay about a mile from the mole and when the gig was half way – an English man of war, opened her ports and saluted the Commodore with eleven guns; at the same time running up the Star Spangled Banner at the fore, which was immediately followed by the others. Then the American flag was seen floating at the fore of seven English men of war and one Brazilian, exclusive of our own. A salute of thirteen guns announced the arrival of the Commodore on board the frigate. As he ascended her side the broad pennant was hoisted at the main, and at the same moment the long coach whip was substituted for the pennant, which until then had floated at the Main of the Decatur. The Potomac now being the flag ship, was entitled to a salute from the other vessels which she received from the Decatur and Enterprise; each firing thirteen guns.

At one, the batteries of our vessels again opened and pealed forth the grand national salute, which was responded to gun for gun by each of the seven Englishmen, the Brazilian frigate, and one of the forts. At two, the Potomac ran up the Brazilian flag at the fore, and saluted the port which was returned by the Brazilian and the fort, and concluded the firing until sundown, at which time a gun from each frigate is fired and as a signal to "down ensigns for the night."

There was not enough wind to raise the smoke above the hull of the vessels after the discharge of their guns, and all that could be seen was the vivid flash of the guns as they followed each other in rapid succession, attended by the thick mass of white curling smoke, which was receiving an addition from every discharge, soon enveloping the tall tapering masts and neatly trimmed yards, in a dense volume of pure white cloud. This was broken only by the occasional flutter of the numerous Star Spangled Banners as they obeyed the impels of the momentary breeze.

The vivid flash of the batteries as they vomited forth their destructive wrath, the majestic curling of the smoke as it rose from the side of these floating citadels, joined the thick mass of clouds above, and the loud report of the many hundred guns, were well calculated to convey to the landsmen a just idea of that awfully grand sight "a great naval engagement" where so many hundreds have fallen and left behind them a name which resounds to all parts of the world, and will out live all the crumbling monuments that posterity can erect to their memory. Thus it was the 4th of July celebration in the harbour of Rio de Janeiro; and now it remains to be told how it was celebrated by myself.

In the first place I must mention that since my arrival, I have taken up my quarters at the "Hotel Phareux", which fronts on the harbour within fifty yards of the principal landing place. In this hotel I am very comfortably situated in room N. 18; in the third story front, with two large windows opening onto a balcony; and commanding an un-interrupted view of the whole harbour. The house is kept by an old Frenchman, in the true Parisian style. The lower room is neatly decorated with large mirrors and hung with numerous paintings. In this saloon a number of small tables are placed, and one can there have whatever they wish, being obliged to pay for no more than they have ordered; so, that no one is obliged to eat anything which does not suit his palate.

On the morning of the 4th, after contemplating for some time from my balcony, the beauties of the surrounding harbour, and admiring the neat trim of the many vessels of war with which the bay was studded, I felt an inward desire for breakfast, and to satisfy that desire I wound my way to the lower saloon, and seated myself before a plate of fresh oranges and bananas, at the same time calling for my morning meal. This I soon disposed of to my entire satisfaction, took a short walk and returned to my room about ten, accompanied by a friend. There we remained, having a fine view of all that was passing in the harbour, until two o'clock, at which time we took a walk as far as the Campo St. Anna.

This is a large plot of ground in the western part of the city, containing about sixty acres, with a few trees scattered o'er it and a large fountain in the centre. Near this fountain a large stone basin is built for the accommodation of slaves who resort there in great numbers to wash clothes; and judging from the crowd of slaves I have always seen here, and the many hundred pieces that are constantly strewed o'er the green, I should say, the basin of the Campo St. Anna was the general "wash tub of the town".

In this campo the troops are reviewed, and during any of their great holy days, booths are erected and all sorts of jugglery and amusement going on, including fire works of every description. In the cool of the morning and evening it is also a place of resort for the ladies, who are carried here in sedan chairs, to enjoy the pure and refreshing breeze that is wafting gently o'er it. This I suppose is called taking exercise, as they are never seen in the street and only leave their residence in closely curtained sedan chairs, or carriages guided by a postillion.

After wandering o'er the Campo and being nearly melted by the scorching rays of a tropical sun, we retraced our steps to the residence of the American Counsel where we had been invited to dine.

At five about thirty gentlemen sat down to a table, which was groaning under the weight and variety of its dishes. It was arranged with great taste and neatness. In the centre stood a large cut glass vase, containing an enormous bouquet of the richest flowers, among which none appeared more handsome than the sweetly blushing rose; at each end a handsome pyramid surmounted respectively with the American flag and Brazilian jack.

The company sat o'er the table for four hours during which time a number of toasts were given and drunk, and a greater number of bottles emptied.

At nine the company retired, and several of us proceeded to a supper, given to the American Naval Officers by an American resident of Rio. At eleven, thirty odd sat down to a magnificent table, well filled with all the delicacies of the season. Here as at dinner, a number of national toasts were drunk, among which our navy and its gallant officers, were favourites, and several national and other songs given. At two o'clock we arose from the table, and in a few minutes, my companion and myself took our departure, well satisfied with our dinner and supper, and feeling the greatest desire to retire to bed and forget the festivities of the day.

I think that by this time, if any one has been so patient as to accompany me thus far, they will be well satisfied to have my scribbling brought to an end, as for fear they might be provoked if I continue to black more paper, I will now cast anchor and bring my pen to a rest, leaving them naught to anticipate, but a very short sketch of my homeward voyage; and promising to those, if any there be, who think I have not fulfilled my promise, to answer all questions they may be pleased to ask, and to communicate much more than is contained in these pages, when I am once more surrounded by my friends, and enjoying the many comforts of home.

(Rio de Janeiro - - July 8th, 1840 --Capital of the Empire of Brazil, South America)

CHAPTER ELEVEN

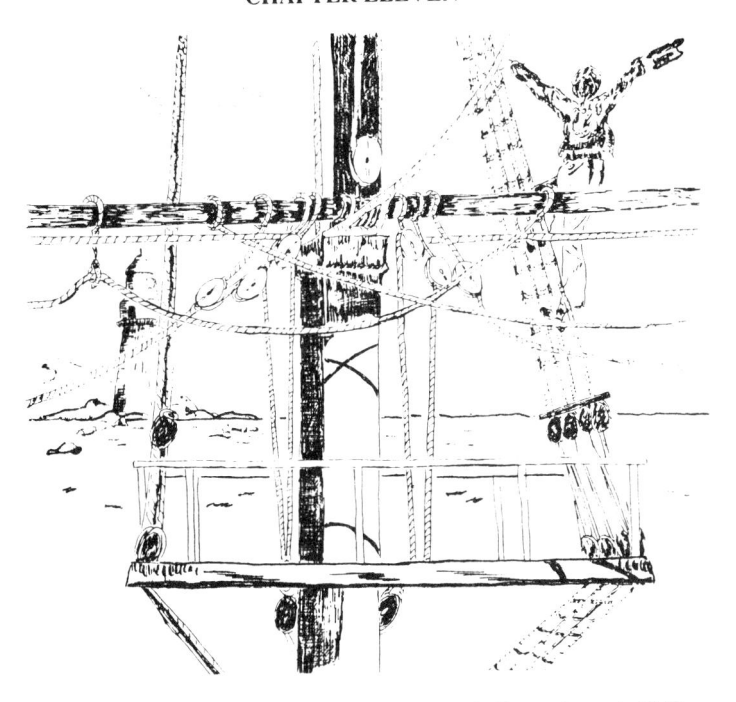

At Sea – August, 1840
"Homeward Bound"

The long wished for day has at length arrived and I am now permitted to head my page with the pleasant, and expressive sentence of "Homeward Bound". It is indeed a pleasant task, but still more so will it be, when I am allowed to close my sea account, and record that our vessel once more rides o'er the water of land, that gave her birth, and that I am again in sight of my boyhood's home.

On the 11th of July the Roanoke was again ready for sea, and at eight o'clock was underway, but owing to a head wind and tide, we had to anchor in the lower harbour abreast of fort Villaganhor, situated a mile beyond the entrance of the bay. The next morning we again got underway, but were as unsuccessful, as the day previous, compelled to anchor in the rolling ground, as it is very properly named, about half a mile outside the entrance. On the morning of the 13th we made a third attempt, our anchor was once more hoisted home, the sails loosed to the breeze, and, as fortune smiled on us with a propitious eye, our gallant little ship, wafted clear of the several islands, which surround the entrance. Long before sun-down, we were free from the rock bound Brazilian shore. Another change has taken place in our cabin, and the place of our passengers from Valparaiso has been supplied by two gentlemen from Rio. One of them is a Dr. Powell of the United States Navy, returning on account of weak eyes, and the other, a Mr. King of New York, who has been acting as Captain's clerk, on board the US Sloop of War, Decatur.

We have also a draft of eight men, sent home from the W.S.Squadron, being invalid and unfit for duty. These men occupy the steerage. Among their number there is one insane man, he is quite harmless and inoffensive, though he requires constant watching, on account of his propensity to displace whatever comes within his reach. At night he is always put in irons, as well as whenever there is any painting going on. Otherwise our crew is the same as when we left Valparaiso with the exception of one boy who ran away while laying at Rio.

How pleasant and delightful it is to look o'er hardships which are past, and loose oneself in the fickle shades of fancy, when picturing the future as filled with bliss and pleasure, and imagining, because soon hard trials have passed, that all our ills are o'er, and whatever follows will be hailed with delight as fraught with naught, but peace and joy. Yet how often, how constantly are such pleasant imaginations nipped in the bud and our fondest hopes blasted when to every appearance, they were in the very act of being fulfilled, and instead of attaining that, we most desire, we are met with thick clouds of disappointment and vexation. How oft does man build on futurity, and assure himself that, that which he most desires will certainly come to pass, and how oft does he meet with a defeat of hopes where he had predicted, may, more, was even confident, of success. And how plain does all this speak and say to mortal man, "though hope is thy anchor, and confidence thy cable, thou can n'er warp thy frail barque as well undertake to move the vast universe, turn the waters to wine, change the course of the winds, or add one to the countless millions of stars that bedeck the luminous heavens, as to struggle for e'en a momentary glance into the vast recesses of futurity.

Never was the truth of this more fully exemplified that it has been since we sailed from Rio. We left the harbour with a head wind, which our all knowing and wise commander was certain would not last more than two or three days, and that after this we must have fair winds, and in thirty days be safely landed in Philadelphia. Of course the shortest time would meet with the best reception from us, and we all fondly hoped that in one month we would bid adieu to the decks of the Roanoke and be snugly moored with our friends at home, after a short and pleasant passage. Yet how soon these fond hopes perished and how plainly was it proven to us, that we know not what a day, or an hour may bring forth. But, to commence our disappointment, the predicted two or three days head wind lasted for fifteen and for eleven we were actually to the southward of Rio, during which time we had a continuation of rains, wind, accompanied with terrific thunder and lightning. One night in particular it was truly awful. All around appeared one mass of impenetrable darkness of the blackest hue.

The rain poured down in torrent, and the sea aroused by the strength of the wind, was combing and breaking in all directions; while every minute the vivid streams of lightning played o'er the bosom of the ruffled ocean, giving its surface an appearance of one vast sheet of fire, and the mighty thunder broke o'er our head with an awful and terrific crash. The darkness of the horizon above, the fire crested waves heaving heavily up, the singing of the blast as it swept through the rigging, the heavy crash of the oft repeated thunder, the singular appearance of the surrounding water spouts, the bright glare of the sharp lightning as it leaped from the clouded canopy that hung o'er us, and the sudden transition from light to dark, attended as it was, by momentary blindness, contributed to raise in my awe struck mind emotions of mingled wonder and fear. I hailed with pleasure and gratitude, the coming of the morn and appearance of the sun, as he mounted up with rapid strides, conquering as he came, until the blackened bow of the previous night disappeared beneath his resplendent rays, and the surrounding horizon was once more gifted with all the attendant beauties of a clear sun-rise.

After these head winds for fifteen days, and beating about the Abrulas Banks for nine more, we took fine breeze and in a few days slipped into the S.E.Trades. We then concluded that all head winds were o'er and that we would have a fine run to the capes. On the 9th of August we crossed Neptune's royal archway, and once more entered the northern ocean. After crossing the line, contrary to all expectation, we were becalmed for eight days. We then took the N.E. Trades in about 11 degrees latitude, and were once more moving through the water as we were used to do. These trades generally extend as far as 28 degrees N. but we are now in 26 degrees and they are diminishing rapidly; so, if the usual bad luck attends us, they will be succeeded by a calm for a week or more.

To add still more to our trials and enhance the laid enjoyment of our voyage, our close fisted captain laid in a very small supply of fresh stock. The whole consisted of six dozen fowls, and three puny little pigs weighing about twenty five pounds each. Of this very limited supply we were so unfortunate as to loose, upwards of fifty fowls, which were killed during the heavy thunder and lightning we had, a few days after leaving port. The few that remained as well as the gutter snipe, were dealt out very sparingly, but soon our scanty table could not boast of even these, and four weeks after leaving Rio, we were reduced to salt provisions. A week or two since, we had the good luck to strike a porpoise. The meat of this sea-hog served as several meals, and, though the steaks would not compare with a rich sirloin or tenderloin, we considered them quite good and were very glad to exchange our salt beef and pork for fresh porpoise steaks.

Few days since, we spoke and boarded an English brig, bound to the West Indies, and obtained from her a few hams. These were also very acceptable and as they were a change, we gladly received them. To say the least of our fare, it has been miserable and contemptible, and well calculated to render our pusillanimous captain, deserving of the highest censure, as he did not actually provide enough for three persons much less sufficient for six.

Those of my friends, who have perused the fore part of this book, will remember my mentioning our having been boarded by an English man of war brig while on our outward passage; and will be surprised to hear, that we have been again boarded by the same vessel, within two hundred miles of the place we before met her. Her last visit was on the 5th of August, in 12 degrees south latitude. She was from Pernambuco, bound to Bahia, and the cause of her commander a few minutes previous to their leaving Pernambuco.

The American Barque, Mary, Capt. Clark from Baltimore; on her passage to Pernambuco, fell in with a suspicious vessel in Lat. 5 degrees N. Long. 27 degrees 10' W. She was a large hermaphrodite Brig, painted black, with a narrow red streak, mounting four long carronades, and a Pivot gun. She chased the Mary for several hours and fired at her until she hove too, and indeed once afterwards, she hailed in Spanish and broken English, ordering the Mary to take in sail. Upon Capt. Clark's demanding what he wanted, he answered," it was none of his business," and to take in sail immediately. Capt. Clark supposes there were at least fifty men on her deck. When first seen at daylight, the stranger had nothing set but a fore spencer, but made sail instantly on discovering the Barque.

A Ship and Barque from the south heaving in sight at the same time as the Barque hove too, caused him to make all sail in an opposite direction, without boarding the Mary. As soon as this information was received we held a consultation, relative to the strength of our arms; and found that among pistols, fowling pieces and a blunder-buss, we can muster about twenty charges, which, if we should be attacked by any of the prowlers of the deep, we shall make use of as long as we are capable of resistance, and always bear in mind the words of Lawrence, "Don't give up the Ship".

To hear of such a vessel as this, seven or eight years ago would not have excited so much surprise; as then it was well known that several piratical vessels, did actually infest the seas, but of late years such a craft has been quite an unusual sight; and may lead us to fear that the same bloody scenes may be again enacted, and many an honest tar sink beneath the cold steel of the lawless pirate. I am in hopes, that this vessel was merely a slaver, who was short of provisions and had turned pirate with no other view than to replenish his stock, and then proceed on his voyage.

During our passage we have amused ourselves in diverse ways; shooting with pistol, fishing, playing back gammon, checkers etc., and performing various gymnastic feats; as well as reading, sleeping, lying about the deck telling odd stories, giving commdrums, and making puns, etc. In fact doing anything that would tend to pass away time. But now we can truly say, that all our sports are o'er, and time hangs heavily on our hands. We have read all our books, worn out all our stories and commdrums, and become satiated with our other amusements. We shall hail with joy the hour when we are permitted to leave the ship, and enjoy the company of others.

Our ship is now a complete paint shop. Paint brushes and pots are flying about in all directions and the oft repeated cry of "take care of the paint", is heard to resound from stem to stern. Every clean pair of pants or shirt (which by the by, are now getting confounded scarce) we put on is sure to be daubed with paint, for if we escape the companionway, the rail is sure to bring us up but if that should give us free, we must inevitably get a touch from some of the rigging, or seat ourselves upon the deck, near where some dauber has been at work. Not with standing all this inconvenience, our ship is looking very clean, and unless we meet with a stress of bad weather, will go into port in first rate order; looking like many of our fashionable families and the lower part of their dwellings, very fine and pleasing to the eye, as far as the outward is concerned. But making a poor meager show within; particularly about meal time, when the deserted table is groaning, not on account of the weight of the numerous dishes, but, for fear, a good puff of wind will deprive it of its cloth, dishes and all, and shock our modesty by exposing the bare boards to our view.

We indulge the fond hope that we may soon be able to leave our scanty table, surrounded only by deserted rooms, which I am sure will furnish sufficient live stock, for subsequent inmates, for some time to come.

We are now in 28 degrees north latitude, and within nine hundred and fifty miles of the Capes (August 28th) which with a fair wind we could reach in one week with the greatest ease. But as luck is evidently against us, and as we are two days doing what any other vessel might in one I suppose we may set ourselves down as within fourteen days sail of port.

For fear however that we might be agreeably disappointed, I think I shall at the Breakwater, (which I am certain will please all my readers, and which I would have pleased me if I could have done so three months since), and overhauling my wardrobe; which I am sure, would draw forth a disinterested person the remark that, my <u>rents</u> were evidently on the increase.

I find there still will be a number of blank pages left, which will not be soiled by my useless scribbling. These I bequeath to my readers, in all their pure, unsullied whiteness, and wish each one to consider that they have an exclusive right to at least one page of my book.

September 3rd we have this fell in with the American Brig, Gabrialacho, from New York bound to Key Sal, West Indies – and were so fortunate as to obtain from her, a barrel of new potatoes and a half barrel of flour. These were indeed a treat to us poor sea tossed souls who had not seen any vegetation for thirty days.

We are now within three hundred and eighty miles of the Capes and though at this moment nearly becalmed, we are in hopes that our potatoes and flour will last us in.

September 9th ----- It is with grateful and pleasant feelings I once more resume my pen and am permitted to record that this long and tedious voyage is now likely to be brought to a close; and I am again in sight of my native land, after an absence of nine months, during which I have experienced six different seasons, and tossed about on the bosom of the raging and tempestuous Sea two thirds of that time, and sailed upwards of twenty three thousand miles.

During the past day we were becalmed within seventy miles of the Capes, and in sight of fourteen sail, all like ourselves, waiting for a wind. About sun-down a moderate breeze sprang up, and our white canvas once more obeyed the impulse of the wind, and was wafting our favourite barque towards the land; when about two bells of the dog watch (7 o'clock) our ears were greeted with the long and anxious expected cry from the lookout man stationed at the mast head, "A pilot boat is bearing down for us off the starboard bow."

This was the signal for a general rush to the starboard side, and in an instant upwards of twenty heads were looming over the rail, all eager to obtain a glance of the truly welcome sight.

In a few minutes a neat, taut rigged schooner run down alongside, rounded too under our lee, and hailed us. Ship ahoy, halloo, do you want a pilot? aye,aye ---lay your main yard aback and we will send on aboard of you. This shout conversation took place between the respective commanders, and in a few seconds a small skiff came alongside, containing the stranger we had so long wished to see; "Little brief Authority", stepped over the rail. The pilot boat then filled away, and we stood on towards the Capes.

At day light this morning we discerned the Light House of Cape Henlopen, and the adjacent land; and at eight o'clock we had the satisfaction to enter the bay with a fine westerly wind; which we have carried as far as Delaware City, where we have this moment (10 o'clock) come to an anchor.

Now, as I am once more in the waters of the Delaware, and this voyage is near a close, I shall bid adieu to my note book, if so you please to call it, and retire to my bed, and dwell upon the sweet anticipation of being in the bosom of my family in the course of the next twenty four hours; where I am sure I shall be recognized as---
　　　　　　　　　　Your Very Obedient Servant
　　　　　　　　　　Benj. Reynolds

# # #